Balancing School and Life and Succeeding at Both

George H. Glade, M.C., M.N., ARNP

HARA
PUBLISHING GROUP

**Published by
Hara Publishing
P.O. Box 19732
Seattle, WA 98109**

Copyright © 2001 by
George H. Glade, M.C., M.N., ARNP

ISBN: 1-883697-86-7

Library of Congress Catalog Card Number:
00-110418

Manufactured in the United States
10 9 8 7 6 5 4 3 2

Editor: Vicki McCown
Cover Design: Richard Van Lê
Book Design & Production: Scott and Shirley Fisher

Table of Contents

Balancing School and Life and Succeeding at Both

Introduction

"The mind is not a vessel to be filled, but a fire to be kindled."

-Plutarch

So, you've been accepted to a college or university. Congratulations. You've got a long and exciting road ahead of you.

Perhaps you are just starting out as an undergraduate. Or maybe you're on your way to graduate or professional school. Has it been a while since you were in a formal educational program? Is there just a touch of nervousness in your stomach about this new chapter to your life? At whatever point you find yourself in your academic career, you know that your acceptance into school means that the bar has just been raised, that the level of expectation, work, and responsibility has just risen.

Don't worry. The apprehension you feel about these new demands merely means that you are normal, especially if you have other commitments to meet. Suppose you have a family and a full- or part-time job in addition to your new academic duties. You may be looking at your life and starting to have doubts. "How am I going to juggle school and work? How will I ever have enough time to spend with my kids, with my spouse, at my job, doing my schoolwork—and keep from ending up needing intensive mental health care?"

I know what that feels like because I lived through that very scenario. While a husband and father, I worked full-time and earned three degrees, two of which were at the master's level. That was quite a turnaround, especially since the first time I went to off to college, I didn't do particularly well.

I was straight out of high school when I enrolled in the University of Vermont, and nothing in my previous academic training had prepared me organizationally to deal with the demands of college. It wasn't that I didn't try; ironically, I probably worked harder at school during this period than at any other time. But try as I might, I couldn't keep up with my workload.

Then fate intervened in the guise of the military and I was drafted into the U.S. Army. In retrospect I can see that it was just what I needed, for two reasons: I got a much-needed dose of what "real life" was like, and I learned how to organize. After that, nothing within the college environment could ever intimidate me again.

When I returned to school, I did very well. While I knew I was bright, I did not consider myself any smarter than my fellow students, although many of them were not doing as well as I. What I want to emphasize is that my academic success came as a result of approaching the task of studying differently—more efficiently—than my peers did.

Frequently people decide that the best way to tackle a difficult task is by doing it more and doing it harder. I know a number of students who tried this method, but they usually ended up exhausted, unable to enjoy the learning process and the academic environment. They cheated themselves out of much of what is exciting and unique about going to school.

I wrote this book because I believe that what I learned along the way can help others enhance their learning experience. This book will strengthen academic performance for the new and returning student, the undergraduate and postgraduate student, and the professional attending technical or trade school.

My wish is that you take to heart the information you find within these pages and, once you have finished with school, that you will look upon this book as having helped you and your family successfully survive a difficult but rewarding time.

If life were to end for either of you, would you want the memory of your last kiss to be that of an impersonal peck? It takes but a moment to make real contact, and it can mean so much.

Love. We all want love in our lives, but what does that really mean? It must start within our own hearts. When you open your heart to increasing the amount and quality of love in your life, you become a source of love. The more love you give, the move love you will receive. Oftentimes, little resentments get in the way of our reaching out. In our petty anger, we wait for our partners (or parents or children) to reach out to us.

The way to be happy is to let go of anger and resentment. Albert Ellis, founder of Rational Emotive Therapy, had a good point. We choose to feel in particular ways. If we hold on to anger, it can grow and take on a life of its own. Small issues take on far more importance than they should. If we choose to be loving, we will receive love in return. Be the first one to reach out. Give flowers or a backrub for no particular reason and without expectation of anything in return. You will receive far more than you give.

If you had one hour to live, who would you most want to be with? No one will live forever. Making love an active part of a relationship involves living in the moment. Live the moments of love in your life in a fully present fashion. Tell each other that you love one another. Show your love in tangible ways. Do the dishes when it's not your turn. Allow your partner to be "right" even if you feel she isn't.

A second part to having a relationship survive is a belief that each of you needs to continue to grow. The sense that you are stagnating is a handcuff that bites into your wrists and restrains your movement. The irony is that, like Dorothy in The Wizard of Oz, who had the power to return home at any time, you have the power right now to change your life, your relationships, and your future. A more realistic Dorothy probably would have throttled the Good Witch for not telling her about this power sooner. Don't wait to accept this truth about yourself. Take the steps to explore those growing edges of your life. Brainstorm how you will support your continued growth through this time. Your partner's focus on school might provide an opportunity for you to grow in ways you have never given yourself permission to explore.

Creating the Ideal Study Environment

"It is singularly ironic that we devote far more effort to develop optimal habitats for zoo animals than we do for our own species."

-Heerwagen et al. (1995)

When zoos were first built, they were nothing like the wonderful animal-friendly facilities we commonly see today. Consisting mainly of concrete cages, they were more like warehouses, confining animals to small, uncomfortable cubicles with little thought for their physical or emotional needs.

In recent years, considerable more care and attention have been given to the housing of animals in zoos, and although they are still confined, their environment is typically much more comfortable and reflective of their natural habitat.

Unfortunately, the same cannot be said about many public buildings, especially those found on college campuses. Even in this day and age, little thought is given to the psychological needs of the people who will use these spaces. Students christen their drab and restrictive cubicles with descriptive and derogatory names: "The Ghetto on the Green," "Castle Cave," and "Shoe Boxes" are a few I recall from my days of dormitory living.

The pictures these places bring to mind are not too far from how these buildings actually look.

This same lack of concern and creativity can be found in the workplace, where the impact of the environment on the workers is often ignored. This disregard for the comfort and needs of people who actually use these buildings stems from the belief that people can easily adapt to their environment. Design focuses primarily on function, providing the bare necessities for performing a task while keeping building and maintenance costs at a minimum. In both academia and the workplace, standardized structures are the norm, with little consideration given to individual differences.

Over the last couple of decades, a new discipline has evolved which explores the impact of the environment on an individual's disposition, development, and production. Environmental psychologists have studied people in a wide variety of work, study, and living environments to see just how much they are affected by their surroundings. Predictably, they found that people seek and prefer environments that are most compatible with their needs and preferences, a condition they term "person-environment congruence." Taking their findings a step further, they also discovered that, when the environment is not compatible nor can be modified to become compatible with an individual's needs, feelings of stress, dissatisfaction, and dissonance often result.

The Negative Environment

An environment can evoke a negative response in its inhabitants in a variety of ways: poor ambient conditions (light, air quality, temperature), noise, crowding, lack of privacy, and the inability to control social interaction are just a few. Let's take a look at the typical college library, an excellent example of the negative environment:

2

1. Poor lighting. Fluorescent lighting, the most common kind used, serves the functional needs of large numbers of people, but does little for the individual as it creates a high-glare work environment.

2. Too hot, too cold. Many libraries have large open spaces with high ceilings, making temperature regulation difficult.

3. Too many people. Crowding is an inherent problem found in the library. Even when not crammed with people, libraries have a constant flow of traffic, contributing to the levels of distraction and noise.

4. No privacy. Library users have little control over social conditions. Private spaces within a library are often difficult to access or nonexistent.

5. Too distracting. The external stimulation in libraries is prevalent and numerous studies find a correlation between an individual's discomfort threshold and environmental stimuli.

6. Too loud. Noise contributes a whole host of negative effects to the learning environment. These include:
   → Decreased cognitive abilities
   → Memory impairment
   → Cognitive fatigue
   → Decreased comprehension on complex tasks
   → Decreased task persistence
   → Stress response of increased physiological arousal
   → Decreased task satisfaction

The Positive Environment

For an example of a positive environment, let's consider the typical home.

Within any home, there are places where people seem to gather. While this may reflect the functional aspects of a room, people are naturally drawn to psychologically compatible spaces. When "person-environment congruence"—as the environmental psychologists call it—occurs, people experience positive feelings, which lead to positive outcomes.

This psychological compatibility is influenced by an individual's perception of an environment as pleasant and inviting. Natural light, particularly sunlight, and a view to the outdoors create a positive perception of spaciousness and decrease a negative perception of being closed in.

Researchers have found that workers in windowless spaces suffer from more negative feelings about their work than their counterparts with windows. A windowless space also affects people's sense of relative time and may throw off their circadian rhythms because they are given no visual cues as to whether it's day or night. In these kinds of work environments, the use of large landscape pictures can sometimes help decrease the perception of being closed in. Lighting can create variability of light and shadow. Reducing visual clutter, lightening the color of walls, and decorating with plants can all enhance the perception of spaciousness.

In the design of a study space, person-environment congruence entails both functional and psychosocial components. The space must fit the needs of the tasks to be performed, be neither too large nor too small, include a desktop large enough to open books and notebooks simultaneously, and be equipped with readily accessible resources. When possible, books, computer access, and phones should be within easy reach of the workspace. Keeping everything needed nearby lessens the chance of becoming distracted and losing focus during study time.

4

Chapter 1 - Creating the Ideal Study Environment

Physical comfort and fit are important, considering the number of hours spent at the workspace. Libraries typically take a "one size fits all" approach to seating. The chair that fits a person who is five feet tall doesn't work well for the person who is over six feet tall. For the private study space, investing in a comfortable chair that suits the individual is a wise expenditure. Having a desk that fits both person and chair is also a must.

What is the ambiance or atmosphere of the room? Is the room a visually pleasant place to spend time in? Ambiance supports both functional and psychosocial congruence. Factors such as comfortable, low-glare lighting, reduced visual clutter, variation in colors and textures in a room, and use of diverse objects increase the spatial interest in a room.

Does the workspace allow the resident to control both privacy and social interaction? The door is one of the truly underrated developments in human social history.

Psychological compatibility is further accomplished by personalizing the study environment. Our territory is often defined by our belongings, as there is comfort in just being around our "stuff." When older adults move to smaller housing, one of the most difficult aspects is parting with their belongings, in effect giving up their unique identity. We decorate our homes in ways that make them pleasant to us. Memories live within both objects and space. Personalizing a new space with our belongings gives us connection with past positive associations and increase our psychological comfort. The new place seems less foreign and more like it belongs to us.

Tips for Creating and Improving Study Space:

→ Arrange furniture so that the phone, computer, and books within easy reach of one another.

→ Put up a bulletin board close to the study area to easily post needed school-related reminders.

→ Choose a study space with a window.

→ Cover crowded bookcases with inexpensive fabric to create visual interest and give the appearance of neatness

→ Erect a screen to cordon off functional but cluttered areas or to create a division when sharing study space with others. Window shutters or fabric screens work well.

→ Drape a couple of yards of inexpensive fabric around a window, softening the hard lines of windows and blinds and adding color, texture, and visual interest to a room.

→ Invest in spotlight-type lamps or upwardly directed floor lamps to bounce light off the ceiling and reduce glare. Can lighting, placed on the floor and surrounded by plants, creates light and shadow and visual interest in a room.

→ Create a large, inexpensive desk with a hollow-core door and a couple of file cabinets. For a more finished look, attach molding to the edges and rub on some stain. Fabric dye can be used to apply more unconventional colors that still allow the wood to show through. Make the surface water- and stain-resistant with spray polyurethane.

→ Bring in plants to make the room seem more alive. Many colleges and universities have greenhouses where students are permitted to take cuttings of unusual plants at no cost.

→ Have on hand a small fan, which circulates the air and provides white noise to mask background sounds, and a portable space heater to accommo date different comfort levels needs when sharing study space.

→ Visit flea markets, thrift shops, yard sales, and hardware stores for objects to add visual interest to a room. Use items in atypical ways. I once had a roommate who used a five-foot piece of sewer pipe as a giant vase for dried plants "harvested" from the campus.

→ Hunt for mismatched sheets at department stores, as they are often inexpensive and make quick slipcovers for beat-up stuffed chairs and couches. A comfortable chair can provide a relaxing alter native from a desk chair when a person has a lot of reading.

→ Stick a "do not disturb" sign along with a notepad on the outside of a dorm room door to reduce distractions.

Notes

Style and Effective Learning

Our entry into the sensory experience of the world literally bombards us with information. Our task at birth is to make sense of that sensory world. As infants we gradually connect that our hands and arms are part of our physical self. As vision clears, we learn that certain faces will nurture us in the variety of ways that are essential to our very survival. Bodily contact becomes associated with the visual cue of the faces of our parents and caregivers. Over time, the sounds of voices take on meaning and an association is made between the visual and the auditory. Words still do not have meaning but the tonality and cadence of the voices of parents and caregivers do. Soon voices become recognizable even in the absence of visual cues, and a touch or a word can comfort an infant's distress even in the absence of visual cues.

The maturing brain progressively becomes more adept at learning to process information received by sound, touch, and vision. We first learn to perceive our world through our senses; as we develop, we begin to identify form and function of those things we perceive. Perceptual learning takes place in the sensory association cortex, with each sense accorded its own spot. The infant develops circuits of neurons which recognize the complex stimuli within the environment, and learning is presumed to be accomplished by changes in synaptic connections.

In the late 1970s, Richard Bandler and John Grinder developed a communication theory which they named neuro linguistic programming (NLP). Their development of this theory was intended for application in psychotherapy, but it can also be helpful in understanding learning style and developing more effective ways of learning.

Bandler and Grinder put forth the theory that our thinking occurs through three main representational systems: creating visual images, hearing sounds, and making sensory contact with the physical world. An individual will use all representational systems, but generally one will become the dominant system used. All of the representational systems operate all of the time, but only part of this information enters consciousness.

Analyzing the creative process can help us understand the concept of representational systems. If you are not musically inclined, ask friends who are how they can remember the notes to play for a piece of music without having the written notes in front of them. When they look at sheet music, how do they translate this to a melody by playing the notes on their instrument? Often these people will describe their experience as one of hearing the sounds in their head.

Have you ever had difficulty quickly deciphering a word when someone spells it aloud to you, and yet you immediately recognize that same word once you see it written? Or think about learning how to find an unfamiliar place—do you prefer written directions or is a map

10

more helpful? Both of these examples reflect the different learning styles which are hard-wired in our brains. More kinesthetically inclined people learn better through tactile experience. Once they play with an object, they know how it works. We have all known children who get into trouble because they seem compelled to touch everything they see. As frustrating as this behavior is for their parents, it is more likely a representation of how that child learns, rather than a sign of disobedience. Touch is fundamental to their ability to process information about their environment—and probably the key to their learning.

You may wonder whether you are oriented visually, auditorily, or a kinesthetically. The truth is, we each employ all representational systems to some extent. No doubt you feel you know which way you learn best. This knowledge can be both a help and a hindrance, for assuming that you learn best one way may limit you from using other systems to support that primary learning method. The challenge, therefore, is to use your strongest process of learning as a pathway to efficiency, but remain open to using the other techniques so that you can learn on as many levels as possible.

I experienced the power of using multiple representational systems in helping my son learn to spell. Spelling presented unique difficulties for him as he had a learning disability that impacted sequencing and pattern recognition. My son would spell words in a shallow pan of rice or a pan of shaving cream, saying the words out loud as he did so. This method used all three representational systems—visual, auditory, and kinesthetic—simultaneously. Once we started using this method, his spelling test scores showed remarkable improvement.

Another method we used that grew from a neuro linguistic programming concept called "anchoring" was "spelling-wrestling." Since we knew that my son's

11

best-developed representational system was kinesthetic, he and I would wrestle in the living room until I had pinned him. To be released, he would have to spell a word correctly. If he didn't spell it correctly, I'd make a loud sound like a buzzer going off and tickle him unmercifully. After a bit of pushing to sound things out, he would spell the word correctly and be released.

My son was always eager to tackle this wrestling approach to learning how to spell. Not only did it help him anchor those spelling words, it provided positive contact and a great deal of fun for both of us. What was once a struggle for him became enjoyable and gave him an opportunity to succeed at a difficult task.

So what is anchoring? Think of Pavlov's famous experiment, where a dog salivated at the ringing of a bell. That is known as stimulus-response conditioning. Anchoring is similar in that it introduces another dimension of sensory experience into the active representational system a person uses, which serves as an "anchor" for the learning taking place. In my son's example, there was a physical, kinesthetic anchor for recalling sequences of letters to spell words. The anchor was a powerful learning tool because of the emotional pleasure of the activity—touching, laughing, and having fun with one of his parents.

We all have experiences in our lives that have been anchored by multiple sensory inputs, some of which were only cognitively experienced with one system. How often have you heard a particular song that evoked memories of a particular time and place in your life? You can remember exactly what you were doing, who you were with, etc. These are anchored experiences. We can use this concept to increase our ability to absorb, retain, and recall information.

Studying chemistry provides a good example of how anchoring can be used to learn. Many students find learning how chemical compounds react to be quite abstract and difficult to grasp. They are left to struggle with learning how to make sense of chemistry by the rote learning of rules for combining things. While rote learning can be useful, even necessary in many cases, learning improves when it moves from the abstract to the tangible.

Chemistry students who need help recalling abstract information can buy inexpensive model sets for building chemical models. As they put together these models, they simultaneously use multiple neurological circuits modules. What is two-dimensional in their textbook becomes three-dimensional in their hands. Now those neuron groups that deal with spatial relationships are brought into play, and this kinesthetic learning element anchors the information in yet another representational model.

13

Years from now, if you have access to a kid's modular building set, you might find yourself making a perfect benzene ring or other complex compound. That's when you will truly know that you have anchored that piece of learning.

Efficiency Learning in High-Fact-Volume Situations

As we have demonstrated, there are many methods for retaining information, all of which require some degree of repetition. By now you probably have an idea which representational system you use best. The key is to find the combination of systems that will let you learn most efficiently.

Let's take the example of trying to retain information from a lecture. Most students take notes to accomplish this, although this approach can actually impede thinking about information as it is given. That's because it is difficult to fully focus on two tasks at the same time. Some students may tape the lecture and then transcribe notes from the tape. This employs both auditory and kinesthetic representational systems but can be fairly labor-intensive. A more efficient plan could be to make flash cards while listening to the taped lecture. Not only do you review the material by making the cards, you can then use the cards to repeatedly review the material.

This type of strategy is often used in successful marketing campaigns. Marketing theorists have developed what is called "the rule of sevens," which states that, to retain a piece of information, the minimum number of repetitions needed is seven. Successful products owe much of their success to the use of repetition of their advertising, rather than their intrinsic value.

14

The same theory can be applied to studying. When the number of repetitions of a piece of information is increased, the ability to recall that information is enhanced.

Many fields of study have a high volume of facts students must be able to recall. Law and medicine are two examples. In the typical anatomy and physiology course, the student will need to memorize in excess of four hundred facts in a typical week. An efficient means of fact repetition is essential.

Flash cards are an excellent tool for achieving high-fact-volume learning. And their effectiveness is not limited to those who learn best through a visual system. Saying the information aloud will help the person who has developed an auditory representational system; and while creating each card, the auditory student can also use the lecture tapes of a lecture as a repetition of the material.

For the person who has a kinesthetic representational system, there are many ways to physically anchor the information. The very act of writing the cards is a physical anchor. Reviewing the cards while performing some physical task, such as walking or riding a stationary bike, is another way to add a physical anchor to the visual stimuli of reading the card. When a student has a tangible structure to remember, like those chemistry molecules mentioned above, reviewing the cards while handling the object is helpful. Having the flash cards handy during lab time, which is often limited, is a great way to get the most out of what you learn in the lab.

What makes an effective flash card? Just putting down the information allows you to review the data, but you want to get more than that for the investment of your time. The design of your cards should reflect your overall strategy for attacking the content of the course, which is usually based on how the instructor tests for the information. In many types of courses, rote reproduction of information is neither how the instructor tests, nor the best way to retain information in long-term memory. Integrating material and understanding relationships allow you to transfer information to other related problems.

Seven Great Tips for Increasing the Effectiveness of Flash Cards

1. Pull not only the facts out of a piece of information, but why the information is important. How will the instructor ask you to integrate the information? Your card should address this.

2. Put only information that you don't know on flash cards.

3. State a question on one side and the answer on the flip side. Phrase the question to closely reflect the

style of the instructor. This question/answer format provides immediate feedback on correct answers which reinforces learning.

4. Color-code an upper corner of the card to easily group cards that are topically related. Learning is enhanced when you review cards with similar topics and concepts.

5. Use highlighters to make key facts or headings stand out. The use of color provides a subtly more complex stimulus, employing the individual modules of neurons of the primary visual cortex, which recognizes color. This broadens the type of neural circuits involved in recall of information. Use several colors of markers to highlight information, using one color on all cards that relate to a particular concept or topic. Resist the temptation to highlight too much; stick to the most important words or concepts.

6. Reproduce diagrams from handouts and textbooks using the copy machine's reduction setting. Paste the diagrams on flash cards, using white-out fluid to remove labels to parts of the diagram. A complete copy can be pasted on the reverse side to allow a question-and-answer format with diagrams. Instructors usually use the same diagram on a test as they did on a handout.

7. Use mnemonics to help recall sequences of concepts. Mnemonics are an excellent way of keying recall for difficult related parts of information.

Mnemonics

A mnemonic, simply defined, is a memory technique based upon association. This type of memory training dates back to the early Greeks and Romans, who associated parts of their speech with parts of their homes.

The opening of the speech would be associated with aspects of the opening to their homes. Parts of the speech would then be associated with a mental journey of the familiar throughout their home. Simonides, a Greek who lived around 500 B.C. and is regarded as the father f the art of trained memory, believed that memory training was important to the further development of the thinking processes.

Our ability to remember relies heavily on association, and much of this association takes place on a subconscious level. For the learner, the task is to make conscious associations with new information that may be intangible or abstract. Remembering becomes easier when the information to be recalled has some meaning in the person's world. After this new information is incorporated into memory and cognitively processed, it takes on meaning and becomes easier to recall.

17

Music provides a good example of the use of mnemonics to assist learning. The lines on the music staff—E, G, B, D, and F—are totally abstract for the beginning student. Initially they have neither relevance nor meaning. Music teachers commonly use the sentence "Every Good Boy Does Fine" as a means of helping students recall the music staff. While the sentence is not familiar, it is understandable. The understandable becomes linked with the abstract, taking the first step of incorporation into memory. Not only do the letters of the music staff become easily remembered, the order or sequence of the music staff becomes easily recalled.

In developing your own mnemonic sentences, the words of the sentence should follow any natural order or sequence that the information has. Anatomy provides many examples of natural order. Take the spinal column, which has five divisions. These are, from top to bottom: the cervical, thoracic, lumbar, sacral, and coccyx. A mnemonic which cues the learner to the names and sequence of these divisions is "Country Texans Love Southern Comfort." The visual learner may naturally form a visual picture of drunken cowboys sitting around sipping Southern Comfort. A mental picture of the mnemonic can further enhance the recollection of the mnemonic for all learners.

When creating a mnemonic device, humor is an important asset. RisquÇ and humorous mnemonics are often recalled for many years. Trying to be amusing and clever in coming up with a mnemonic also adds an element of fun to the task of learning.

Many fields of study have published books of mnemonic devices. While it can be fun to invent your own, sometimes it's a relief to have it already done for you. A book of some topic-specific mnemonics is a good investment.

The following is a list of resources on mnemonics from a variety of fields.

Demonic Mnemonics: Eight Hundred Spelling Tricks for Eight Hundred Tricky Words. by Murray Suid.

Fritz Spiegl's Sick Notes: An Alphabetical Browsing Book of Medical Derivations, Abbreviations, Mnemonics, and Slang for the Amusement and Edification. by Fritz Spiegl.

Vocabulary Cartoons: Building an Educated Vocabulary With Visual Mnemonics. by Sam Burchers et. al.

Medico Mnemonics: A Collection of Fun, Ribald, Irreverent and Quite Witty Mnemonics for Medical Students. by E. S. Marlowe

Memory Notebook of Nursing: A collection of Visual Images and Mnemonics to Increase Memory and Learning. by Zerwekh et al.

Mnemonics for Anatomy Students: a Guide to Memory Aids for the Student of Anatomy. David J. Gerrick

Mnemonics, Rhetoric and Poetics for Medics Vol. 2. by Carolyn PedleyPocket

Pocket Mnemonics for Practitioners. by Robert L. Bloomfield, E. Ted Chandler

Psychiatric Mnemonics and Clinical Guides. David J. Robinson

Pict-O-Graphix: Mnemonics for Japanese Hiragana and Katakana. by Michael Rowley

Pict-O-Graphix: Over 1,000 Japanese Kanji and Kana Mnemonics. by Michael Rowley.

Waspleg and Other Mnemonics. by Bart L. Benne

The Great Memory Book. by Karen Markswitz and Eric Jensen

Blueprints for Memory; Your Guide to Remembering Business Facts, Figures and Faces. by William D. Hersey

The Art of Memory. by Francis A. Yates

Notes

Organization and Efficiency

The more demands you have on your time, the greater is your need for organization. Organization allows you to both keep track of all those many demands each day places on you and to efficiently address them as well. For all of us who are trying to cram ad much as we can into a twenty-four-hour day, organization is essential.

I have noticed that people often define themselves as inherently organized or disorganized. Such an observation stems from a belief rather than irreversible reality. A belief system can be changed, simply by experiencing success within a new belief system. The truth may be that you simply don't have the tools you need to become organized. This chapter is about getting the right tools and creating a new belief system. You can be an organized person!

A good place to start your reorganization is with an analysis of your environment. Look around. Does your study space suffer from excessive clutter? Time to throw out the notion of organized chaos; admit that you don't know where everything is in that mess. If you have stacks of papers, even if they are sorted, all you have are stacks of sorted papers. And even when you get around to shuffling through those stacks of papers, what's the point if you have no place to put them once they are organized?

You need a place to store things. Invest in a file cabinet and a box of dividers (about $50 in most areas). Give some thought to other tools you will need, such as a daily calendar on which you can write your agendas and an easy-to-use rolodex. Buy everything you need in one shopping trip.

Once you have your equipment in place, you can put into practice the guiding principle for keeping your desk organized: The first time you touch a piece of paper is also the time you act on it. This is another way of saying that you never want to touch the same piece of paper twice. This may sound unrealistic given the demands of a student, but it can be done.

Take an action-oriented approach to keeping clutter out of your workspace by following my...

Top Ten Tips to Organize Your Work Space

1. Set up a filing system that allows you to access information quickly and easily. Label files with short, generic names; don't be too specific or you will end up with a whole lot of files, many with very little in them. Avoid giving into the impulse to label one file "Miscellaneous," which translated means "disorganized collection of things you won't readily be able to find." Before you know it, it will have grown too fat with dissimilar information, defeating the purpose of your filing system.

2. "When in doubt, throw it out." This adage has been around for a long time, and it is just as true now as when the unknown efficiency expert created it. We all have heard the horror stories about mothers who threw out childhood collections of Barbies and baseball cards that are now selling for a fortune on the Internet. Still, I suggest you take this saying to heart, because it offers some good advice. If you can't file an item, and can't figure out some specific future need for it, best to get rid of it.

3. Use a day-timer or calendar to record meetings, appointments, and other time-sensitive information. I've heard more than one person say "My brains are in my calendar." Ironically, those are the people I consider to be smart, for they don't clutter their minds trying to remember some appointment in the distant future. With a day-timer or pocket calendar, you have everything you need to organize your time at your fingertips. No more looking for that scrap of paper on which you hastily wrote down an appointment time, no more scheduling an appointment only to realize later that you have a conflict. With a day-timer, you have better control of your time, which saves you time.

4. Devise a system for paying bills in a timely manner. One way to do this is to file a bill as soon as you receive it with other bills you will pay at the same time. Or you can mark its pay date on your calendar. For those of you who want to stick with the "touch it only once" practice, pay it when you open it. That way, you will never be delinquent on a payment, which can carry a stiff penalty.

5. Keep your library of information up-to-date. For example, if an acquaintance calls you with a new phone number or address, immediately make the change in your rolodex or address book. I had the

habit of keeping business cards and bits of paper with friends' phone numbers stuffed in my wallet. Not only did it take me a while to locate a number when I wanted it, my wallet eventually became too large to fit in my back pocket.

I haven't broken myself of the habit completely, but now I periodically clean out the cards and scraps of paper and put them where I can readily access them. With business cards, I staple them right to the rolodex card. I also note the context in which I acquired a card for those I feel might not be self-evident. I can, of course, recall who my friends are; the same may not be true of someone I meet at a party or a seminar. When someone calls whom I have met only briefly, I simply spin my rolodex to their name and instantly recall who he or she is, take in the background information on the card, and jump right into the conversation. People are generally quite pleased that I have remembered them, even though our previous contact was minimal.

When you organize all the information about the people you know in one place, you not only save yourself time, you create a tremendous network which can be useful to you for years to come. Classmates, professors, advisors, friends, colleagues, mentors, coaches, teammates, professional peers —all of these people are worth having in your address book or rolodex. They may be invaluable to you when it comes time to look for work in your field.

6. Deal with incoming correspondence in one of two ways: either file it away for future reference or assign a time to respond to it. I find that the best time to answer letters is after I have finished with any school-oriented work for the day. Writing to friends or family takes less effort than studying. And writing personal letters provides a more satisfying end to the day.

24

7. Reduce your clutter by keeping books and magazines organized on the bookshelf when not actively in use. Periodicals provided by an instructor can be filed in the class notebook, and the notebook shelved as well.

8. Get rid of magazines that are more than two months old. Consider donating them to a place where others will enjoy reading them. Nursing homes, the gym, the library, even local jails are just a few places that can use recent magazines. If the magazine contains something you want to retain, put the information in a computer file or file it away in the appropriate file.

9. Respond to school- or work-related messages at the first reasonable interval in your school work. Incorporating this task with a planned break lets you accomplish two objectives simultaneously. Wait until the end of the study period or day to answer social calls.

10. Keep a neat, well-organized desk, for it is the spring board to overall organization. Give some thought to how you want to set up your study place. For example, a rack above or next to your desk where you can store items you'll want at hand for your studies that day will help keep you focused on your assignment. By gathering everything you'll need in one, convenient spot, you won't be constantly interrupting your work to get one more thing.

Organize the Day

Planning your day is essential to keeping yourself organized and on track; making a list is the most efficient way I've found to do it. When you write down what you want to accomplish during your day, you can better prioritize the list of tasks. You will also save yourself time by seeing which tasks can be batched together. An added benefit is that your memory is prompted to remember

25

various tasks specifically because you put them down in black and white.

And don't overlook that satisfying feeling that comes with crossing off those tasks on your list that you have completed. When you can physically see what you have done during the day, your time and efforts become more tangible, and you are left with a sense of real accomplishment.

The best time to create a list is either at the beginning of the day or at its end, in preparation for the next day. Your list will develop from two sources. The first source consists of those tasks that evolved from your activities during that day which need to be addressed either the next day or soon after. The second source is your daily calendar, where you have already scheduled important items you need to act on.

As your life becomes more complex, the daily to-do list will get longer. Implementing a few minor organizational strategies will save you time and effort. First, as mentioned above, group similar tasks together and do them all at once. For example, in one sitting, you can make all your phone calls; open and read mail; pay bills or take care of correspondence. In other words, batch those tasks together which can be intermingled because of their natural relationship.

This kind of planning is even more important when you're out running errands. Make as few trips as you can and plan the most efficient route. When out shopping, don't forget to have a list of everything you need so you don't have to make an additional trip for forgotten items.

One of the most important organizational strategies you can use is very simple: finish one task before you start another. Of course, sometimes a project is so extensive that it can not be finished in one session. In those cases, break the project down into smaller steps, then systematically complete each step before you move onto the next. For example, gathering resource papers, reading and note-carding, and writing a first draft are natural steps for completing the larger task of writing a term paper. You work on the larger project a little at a time, always making progress toward the completion of the larger project.

Organize the Academic Period

If organizing the daily schedule provides the close-up picture, organizing the quarter or semester gives the panoramic view. The goals are similar to those in organizing your day: to keep you on track with the needs of the entire academic period. This broader scope of organization allows you to establish priorities and set deadlines within the big picture of everything you need to accomplish during that period.

27

The starting point for this organizational plan comes during the first week of school, when course outlines, which include papers, tests, and other expected work for the class, are given. Once you have received all of the course syllabi, you are ready to start developing the big picture of your tasks for the quarter or semester.

Remember that large calendar I suggested you buy, the one with lots of room for you to write on each day? Take that calendar and write down all of the test dates, term paper due dates, project due dates—anything with a deadline that you must meet. A bright color of ink will make these due dates really stand out on the calendar; color-coding the tasks is even more helpful.

Next, break down larger tasks into their natural, smaller steps and assign completion dates for each of these steps. For papers, you will need to gather reference materials, read and process the materials, and write a final draft. To alleviate the pressure of deadlines, assign a completion date at least a week prior to the due date. This can save you a great deal of stress, and with the widespread availability of personal computers, you should easily be able to make any last-minute corrections or additions that may grow out of the lecture.

Preparing for a test takes essentially the same path as the steps involved in writing a paper. Break down the larger job of preparing for a test into smaller, more manageable tasks. Here are a few questions that will help you get organized:

→ How many times do you need to review material for a particular course to prepare for a test?
→ Does the lecture depend on you having completed the reading? If this is the case, schedule your reading time before the lecture.
→ Are you going to have study sessions with others? These, too, can be scheduled at the beginning of the academic period.

Schedule some time on the day before a test for an overall review of the materials to be covered. Don't leave this last and most important task until the day of the exam. Last-minute cramming is not nearly as effective as a methodically developed process of study, and it can make you feel rushed and anxious. When you maintain your steady, step-by-step study plan, you are more focused and retain information better.

When should you plan on studying for a particular course? The answer is before the lecture. This may sound strange, but it goes back to the idea of clumping similar tasks together. You read the material, and then you hear the professor lecture on that same material. These complementary strategies make learning more integrated as ideas from reading are echoed in the lecture

for a course. A higher degree of retention and comprehension is possible because the material becomes anchored in multiple representational systems—in this case
visual and then auditory.

I suggest adding what and when you plan to study
to that big calendar. Again, use distinctive colors, ones
that are different from those you've already used to
designate exams or papers. At this point the organization
of the term really starts to tighten up and take shape; you
can see exactly what you'll being doing as you progress
through your courses. Remember, all this organization is
simply a tool to keep you on track and making consistent
progress toward a particular goal.

While organizational strategies for writing term
papers or preparing for tests have many similarities, they
also have some important differences. Tests measure a
student's mastery and recall of information presented a
number of times, generally during a series of lectures. A
term paper reflects a student's ability to develop and
integrate related information often gathered outside the
lecture. Steps required in preparing for a test are frequent
and repetitious in nature; steps taken to write a paper are
usually not repetitive but more extensive in nature.

29

Over the years, I developed a useful pattern that
helped me accommodate both styles of preparation.
During the week (Sunday through Thursday), I worked
on lecture and test preparation, which allowed me to take
advantage of subject-specific strategies to learning. On
the weekend (Friday through early Sunday), I put the
weekly materials aside and focused on paper preparation,
taking advantage of the fact that the library was less
crowded during this time. Of course, I found there were
times when I couldn't stick to this schedule, and being
flexible was important. But, for the most part, this separa-
tion of tasks worked well, and had the added advantage of
alleviating the feeling that I had to do everything at once.

Once I'd plotted my course, I used the calendar feature on my personal computer to produce calendars for each course of the academic period. I then placed the calendar with test and term paper due dates in front of each course's notebook for that course. This provided an additional—and handy— reminder of the demands of a particular course.

While the organizational strategies I've outlined above are important in addressing the demands of school, there are a number of easy, straightforward ways of saving time and becoming more efficient—in school and life. Here is yet another Top Ten List.

Top Ten Time-Savers for Academic Efficiency

1. Use your waiting time! The day is full of spaces of time where you must wait—but it doesn't have to be lost time. Get in the habit of carrying something with you to read. I often reviewed flash cards during the down time in between periods of hockey games. Whether it's flash cards or a book or lecture notes, keep something you need to read handy. Not only will you put that otherwise wasted time to use, you'll lessen the frustration that comes from waiting.

2. Minimize schmoozing time. It is easy to get distracted by friends, especially when you're looking for an excuse not to do your work. Social time offers an important component in keeping your life balanced, but you don't want it to interfere with your study time. The solution is to combine your socializing with lunch or dinner breaks. When you do this, the time you spend with your friends becomes valuable, high-quality time. Making a lunch or dinner date with friends gives you something to look forward to, a reward for your hard work. The conversation will not only provide you a needed break from your studies, it will actually help to slow down your eating, which

makes a meal more enjoyable and healthy. When I share a meal with friends, we make it a rule to talk about something other than our work or studies, instead focussing on just enjoying one another's company. I always come away feeling relaxed, renewed, and ready to get back to work.

3. Schedule your recreation time. The old saying "All work and no play makes Jack a dull boy" is true. It's easy to get so consumed by an exam, project, or paper that we neglect our important relationships. Planning to spend time in enjoyable pursuits, with family or by yourself, is fundamental to sustaining yourself through the rigors of academia and life. Recreational activities will leave you feeling refreshed and rejuvenated, much like recharging your battery, and help put your schoolwork into proper perspective. Failing to make time to relax and have fun is a sure prescription for burnout and resentment of school, both of which decrease your effectiveness as a student.

4. Prevent needless interruptions. Stick a sign on your door that says you are unavailable till a specific time, such as 10 p.m. Use your answering machine like you would a secretary: Let it pick up the calls so you can screen them, leaving all but the most urgent for a call-back at a later time.

5. Study when you are at peak efficiency. Don't try to work late into the night after a long, hard day. It's far better to get up earlier the next morning and put in study time at the beginning of the day, when you are fresh. Determine what time in the evening is a good stop time for you. Use the time before going to bed to wind down or return social calls, if it's not too late.

6. Limit your time watching TV (or just shoot it!). Use TV as wind-down time, not as your main form of

recreation or an excuse to avoid your studies. There is nothing on TV as important as creating your future by successfully advancing your education.

7. Invest in the tools to properly do the job at hand. Although the initial cost may be higher than you'd like, you will find it to be money well spent. The right tools will save you time and effort and, yes, money by helping you organize and manage your workload.

8. Use those services available that will help you produce a better product in less time. If you are a terrible typist, pay someone to type papers or at least clean up your rough draft—easy to do nowadays with computer disks. Graduate students often provide help in critiquing and proofreading papers for a fee, and some schools will pick up the tab for this service so that there is no cost to the student. Check with the department secretary, other students, or school bulletin boards to find help in this area.

9. Learn how to take in information quickly and efficiently. Many professors seem to suffer from the delusion that their course is the only thing—or certainly the most important thing—that you have going on in your life. In an attempt to share all there is to know on their subject, they will assign an overwhelming amount of reading. You can't always predict which professor will do this; the number of credits for a course may be a poor indicator of the amount of reading and preparation for a course. As always, a student should endeavor to read whatever material a professor has assigned. However, when you find yourself faced with more reading than you can manage, try this strategy: For all recommended readings, read the first paragraph of the piece, which introduces the overall subject; followed by the first sentence of successive paragraphs, which will cue key points; and ending with the summary, which should

32

reiterate the relevant and significant points of
the material.

10. Organize your work and living spaces. Messes are not
just inefficient, they are tiring. If instilling
organization means you are faced with large-scale
revamping of your living spaces, start with areas that
bother you the most. Do a little bit every day; even if
you clear off just one tabletop, you've taken a step
toward getting the job done—and you will reap the
benefits of a neat and orderly environment.

Balance

Even with the best-laid plans, events in our lives
do often not follow our agenda. Our families are seldom
working from the same plan we are. Children have an
especially difficult time understanding that their parent
is too busy to spend time with them, and they suffer hurt
and disappointment. On the other hand, parents who
are students find themselves overburdened by their
studies, their job, and their family responsibilities;
naturally they can become resentful and short-tempered
at interruptions.

The irony is that rigidly sticking to the agendas
we set for ourselves may generate more pressure than is
necessary. From the perspective of a child, a parent
who is inflexible, who must stick to the initial plan no
matter what, appears unavailable and unresponsive to
the child's needs. In turn, children will both hide their
disappointment and act out their anger. This behavior
is an accurate barometer for the tension that the parent
is experiencing.

An agenda should be viewed as a guide or an ideal
of what you would like to accomplish. Childhood doesn't
wait. Special moments pass in an instant and are forever
lost if not experienced as they happen. There are, of

33

course, times when you have to get a certain amount of work done. You must have time when you are fully present and focused on your work, just as you need time to be fully present with the important people in your life.

Creating balance in your life while contending with the demands of school is a difficult task. You may want to plan starting your day with high-quality time with your family. This can be as simple as sitting down to breakfast together. Then, negotiate the time you need to do your work. And, finally, finish up the day again with the people you care about.

After all, school is not the end-all, be-all of life, but rather a transition time. Inner balance comes from maintaining contact with the people in our lives who sustain us. Learning how to be flexible and let go of our rigid agenda allows us to stay in contact with what is truly important in our lives.

Organization is a tool that helps us to accomplish our goals. It is not our master.

34

Developing a Writing Style

The academic period begins, and the tension starts to build, much like it does in a horse race, except you are the one at the starting gate. As you look down the stretch, you see several term papers—like so many hurdles to jump—that you will have to develop, research, and finally compose during this academic period. Perhaps you have done well up to this point in your writing efforts; now, however, whether you are just starting college or are proceeding on to graduate or professional school, you realize the level of expectation has been raised.

Understandably, you might be a bit apprehensive. Not only will your work have to be better, you will have stiffer competition from other students. Your instructor will read numerous papers during the academic period. Chances are, only a few will stand out from the crowd both in form and content. Your goal is to create a finely crafted paper that not only clearly communicates critical thought—a skill acquired through diligence and practice—but is professional in its presentation. You can achieve the latter simply by neatly typing the paper on good-quality bond paper, using an easy-to-read black font to reduce the instructor's eye strain, and making sure that the spelling, grammar, and punctuation are correct.

In the competitive world of education, your paper makes a powerful statement about you. When your paper stands head and shoulders above the crowd, you reap more than just a good grade; you distinguish yourself in the eyes of your instructor. When professors are presented with various opportunities for students, they pass them on to those whom they perceive as the most capable. When you submit written work that is complete and well-presented, your teachers will hold this opinion of you.

Basic Tools

A starting point for every student is to acquire those basic tools essential to producing good writing. First and foremost in your toolbox should be an understanding of your school's library system. Being able to readily find the information you need is critical to your success as a writer. This means you must also have a command of the library's computer system so you can easily search for references. If you choose to avoid acquiring these skills, you will waste precious time looking for what you need and limit your realm of resources.

Libraries offer orientations both to the library and the computer systems in use in that library. Commit to learning these systems in the first week of school, and mark it down as a task on your calendar. In addition to their main library, many large colleges and universities may have several other libraries, each with a specific focus, such as law, medicine, or social work, and with their own unique systems. If your course of study takes you into a specialized library, orientation to that library is also essential.

Since you can't be at the library whenever you work on your writing assignments, you must develop a reference library of your own. Start by selecting a good college-level dictionary, one that has a minimum of 150,000 entries. Use it often, not only to check your spelling but to explore new words and expand your vocabulary.

A second essential is a thesaurus, which comes from a Latin word meaning "treasure house." This treasury of synonyms will help you discover a new word, inject a certain nuance, or just make your writing more precise, accurate, interesting, and varied. Although its choices will be more limited, the thesaurus feature on a word processing program provides the same kind of help at the push of a button. If you find that you are repeating a word in your writing too frequently, use the thesaurus feature to suggest alternatives. For example, for the word "alive," Microsoft Word gives the following synonyms: having life, in a living state, animate, breathing, living, vital, active, mortal, and existing. Using a variety of descriptive words gives a written work more texture and vitality.

Another useful tool is a publication manual. Often, instructors will designate a writing format that they wish the student to follow, and a publication manual will show you how to present your information in that format. Even if the instructor does not indicate a particular writing format, investing in this guide is still a worthwhile expenditure. Publication manuals assist the student in reducing the bias in language, give instructions for presenting statistical information, and delineate the standard on how to reference everything from personal communications to items from the Internet. The most common format used for the social sciences and medicine can be found in:

Publication Manual of the American Psychological Association, 4th edition.

This is available on the Internet at:
http/www.ling.lu.se/persons/Marianne/texts/
APAguidelines.html

A guide on writing style is a great help to anyone who must write. There are lots of good ones out there, but one in particular has served writers of all kinds for several decades and has become the definitive publication on style. It is:

Strunk, William, Jr. and White, E.B. The Elements of Style (3rd ed.) New York: Macmillan, 1979.

Another useful book is:

Turabian, Kate L. Student's Guide for Writing Research Papers (3rd ed.)Chicago: University of Chicago Press, 1976

This last book is both brief and to the point while providing valuable insights on what it takes to write a top-quality paper. Regarded as a classic in its field, this guide is just as useful and relevant now as when it was first published.

Good writers are not born, they develop. Good writing requires not only effective techniques but continued practice supported by the proper tools. The books mentioned here are essential to the success of any student entering higher education. Keep in mind that academic writing differs from creative writing; it is more defined and can be extremely demanding. You may have to make a few changes if academic writing is new to you. With the help of these books, your transition will certainly be smoother.

Accessing Help in Learning to Become a Good Writer

I have found that instructors readily support those students who are intent on improving their writing skills. You would be wise to let your instructors know that this is one of your goals and share with them any concerns you have about your writing ability. Many teachers keep a file of previously submitted papers which they consider to be of exceptional quality, and they will usually let you read those papers if asked. Being able to review what an instructor regards as good work gives you a better understanding of the standards and perceptions of that instructor.

If a professor does not have a such a file, you may instead be referred to a former student who stood out as an excellent writer. Again, getting tips on writing for that particular professor can be a great help to you. Don't be afraid to ask for what you need! No one knows what that is but you, and I think you will find that most people will be willing to help.

Usually, instructors will include guidelines and requirements when they hand out an assignment, often being very specific. Follow these to the letter, as they will certainly relate to the grade evaluation process. If you are asked to give eight references, then give at least eight references! If it's a struggle to find the required number, you may have to be creative. For example, look at what references were cited by those periodicals you used. The authors had to get the information to support their paper from somewhere, and you can list those references as well.

Let the required elements direct you on how to write the paper. In fact, you can use them to divide your paper into sections and create logical headings for those sections. I cannot stress enough the importance of section headings. They are the road signs of a paper's content. A well-marked, easy-to-navigate paper is easier to follow than one that gives no direction, and a professor who must wade through several papers will appreciate your organization. Section headings point the way, revealing methodical study and leading to a sound conclusion. Using headings also helps you to think in a logically organized manner, which will greatly aid you in writing papers when you do not have the advantage of specific requirements.

If you turn your papers in before their due date, instructors or their graduate students may be willing to review them and give feedback. The paper should be as good as you can make it—what you consider a finished, final copy. Ask them to be critical in their evaluation, and then be prepared for the possibility of receiving more—and sometimes more critical—feedback than you expected. Sometimes what you will hear from people whom you admire is pretty darn humbling. The critiques I received on my first papers left me feeling that I didn't know anything and certainly didn't belong in college. However, since hustling tables or working on the assembly line didn't hold much appeal, I just kept at it. And, eventually, I got the hang of it.

What helped me greatly was that I kept reminding myself that the goal was to develop excellence in my writing style. I came to understand that doing so is a process. I repeat, BECOMING A GOOD WRITER IS A PROCESS! The process and the struggle will push you to improve. Don't expect to start out a great writer; do expect to work hard, pitch a lot of wadded-up pieces of paper in the trash can, and to persevere until you are satisfied with your work. You owe yourself the pursuit of excellence. If you want to grab that brass ring of the best that life has to offer, you must demand that you give your best effort.

40

Deciding What to Write About

An instructor assigns a paper with no specific guidelines and confined only by the nature of the subject you are studying. At first you think this is great; you can write on whatever you like. Yet, when you sit down to actually tackle the task, no thunderbolt of inspiration strikes you, no burning question demands to be answered, not even a tiny glimmer of an idea pierces what seems to be a great, dark, empty space between your ears. You are stuck and you haven't a clue as to how to become unstuck.

Don't despair—it has happened to everyone who's ever had to put pen to paper, or fingers to keyboard as more often is the case today. Here are a few strategies to help you prime the pump.

A good departure point is to consider what interests you. The assignment will seem less difficult and overwhelming if you can combine it with an area of interest to you. By steering the assignment toward what you like, you will create an enthusiasm which naturally makes the actual writing easier. If you still need some help, try looking through the list of the assigned books for the class.

The next step takes you to the library where you can probe the data base. Very few ideas exist that haven't already been considered by someone. Enter key words to perform the data search. Think of it as throwing out a wide net to see what you can reel in. Sometimes the catch will be only other key words. Often it provides a flood of references. Examine these references to refine exactly what you want to write about. Take into account how much literature exists on a particular topic. If there is very little, the topic may be too obscure or unimportant. If there is quite a bit, the subject may have been done to death. Still, that may not deter you from tackling a popular idea and giving it an update by citing more recent information.

Newer students often fall into the trap of overenthusiasm, tending to bite off more than they can chew. Remember, a ten-page paper is not War and Peace. A paper can suffer from both being too general or too specific. The goal is to strike the right balance and remain within the stated requirements.

Once you determine what you want to write about, find a general article on the subject. References to general articles can be found in books and other articles on your chosen subject. Perusing these references also provides a great way of finding collections of related articles, which may springboard onto another, more fascinating topic you want to pursue. Perhaps the best source of general articles is an encyclopedia, because the information is specifically written to be general in nature. Once you've located a general article, read through it to decide whether this topic truly interests you. You want to narrow the focus of your paper as well as find something relevant to the course. Perhaps most important, you want a topic that has a ready supply of available research.

The Six Essential Approaches to Purpose

Once you've defined your topic, you're over that initial hump and you can wipe the sweat from your brow. But don't get too complacent, as that next hump awaits. It's not enough to know what you're going to write about. You must have some idea of how you're going to write about that subject.

To get started, ask yourself this question: What is the purpose of writing about this topic? The answer will become the lead section for your paper, the rationale for why you are spending valuable time, effort, and energy to write about it. There are six common ways to approach presenting the purpose of a paper.

1. Comparison. Comparison takes two or more elements of a topic and examines both the similarities and differences. This is by far the most popular approach, as it is simple, straightforward, and familiar. Comparison is relatively easy for the writer to employ and for the reader to understand. Some examples of are:
    A. Methods of doing things
    1) Autocratic vs. Laissez faire management
    2) Using high demand study techniques vs. Winging it

    B. Types of treatment
    1) Psychoanalysis vs. Cognitive-behavioral therapy
    2) Pain relievers vs. Massage

    C. Belief systems
    1) Christian vs. Moslem religions
    2) Republican vs. Democratic platforms

2. Description. This approach reviews and summarizes the research of other people. The topic is divided into its elemental parts, and each is examined based on existing information. Integration of the topic comes from a discussion of why these parts are meaningful or relevant to the subject. Example: Literature reviews.

3. Chronology. In this strategy, the evolution of a subject over a period of time is explored. The integration of the topic comes from a discussion of the factors that brought about change. Example: Change in public policy regarding capital punishment.

4. Questions. This method asks "How should things be?" It can and often does utilize elements of the

other strategies, such as a comparison of pros and cons on an issue or a chronology of the evolution of divergent positions. The goal is to provoke thought on an issue. Example: Should medical use of marijuana be permitted?

5. Persuasion. This is the more aggressive twin of the question technique. Here the writer holds a position on the topic and puts forth an argument to support that position. The strength of the argument depends on solid evidence and sound logic, but it is often the ability to write compellingly that wins the day. The writer can be disarmingly charming or as tenacious as a bulldog—whatever it takes to convince the reader. Talented persuasive writers can find huge financial rewards in working for political campaigns, advertising agencies, and lobby groups. Example: The necessity to legalize medical use of marijuana. (Note the difference in emphasis in the presentation between the "question" and "persuasion" approaches on the same topic.)

6. Analysis. In this approach the writer introduces research or evidence to support and explain a premise that is presented as fact. Some questions that might be answered in this approach are: What are the factors influencing the issue or topic? How are they interrelated? What are the researchers' conclusions and how are they supported by facts? Example: The demise of social security.

While these approaches offer very different methods for tackling your assignment, you'll find that, in practice, you will draw upon all of them. Still, certain disciplines use some approaches more often than others. For example, if you're a law student, analysis and persuasion are most likely the types of approaches that will be useful in your future profession. The ability to accurately use description is an essential skill in medical professions.

Sales and marketing rely heavily on persuasion and comparison.

Sometimes the papers you write while in school seem irrelevant to your future. When you can look down the a road a bit and realize that the writing skills you're developing now will serve you well later on, you can see the value of school as a training ground for your future profession.

The Writing Process

Your instructor has set the guidelines for your paper, and you have determined the topic. The next step is to focus on the sections and flesh out an outline for each. You can do that by practicing some creative brainstorming.

45

Start with a large piece of paper. Large-sized computer print-out paper works well and usually can be found in the recycle bin. In the center of the paper, write a brief statement of the problem or idea to be discussed in your the paper. Phrase it in a manner consistent with your approach to the purpose of the paper. Next write the sections you or your instructor want considered in the paper so that they orbit around the center statement.

Webster's defines "brainstorming" as "the unrestrained offering of ideas and suggestions." "Unrestrained" is the key concept here, as you want to let your imagination run wild while developing the facets of each section. Write down everything that comes into your head, even those ideas that seem stupid or silly. Without the ability to see the silly, it's harder to develop the sensible. This exercise is the fuse that lights the creative process.

Consider putting down your thoughts in question form, as one question can provoke more questions, which in turn will lead to more ideas. What develops is not unlike ripples spreading out from a stone thrown into a still pond. You are creating a range of ideas that all lie within a single visual field.

The next step is to draw lines between related ideas. This is the glue that binds together the ideas from different sections of the paper, illustrating the connection of concepts and demonstrating the integration of the material in a paper.

Now shift out of your anything-goes, right-brain creativity into a more reasoned, left-brain analysis. Transforming the outcome of your brainstorm into an outline is your next step. The outline provides both clarity and focus to the process of writing, keeping you organized and on track in producing a paper that presents a logical progression of ideas.

Group together related thoughts that apply to a particular facet of the topic. Use highlighters to do this quickly and effectively. During your brainstorming, critical evaluation was put on hold. Now it comes into play, culling the best ideas from the many you have jotted down.

The largest section of the outline consists of the major points you will discuss. Start by referring to the guidelines for what the instructor considers the critical elements of the paper. If these are vague, check your references to see how other writers have treated the organization of their papers or articles. Include the largest elements in your outline.

The traditional form for outlines is as follows: Roman numerals for the major elements; capital letters for the first-level subheading; Arabic numbers for the next level; and lower case letters for the last level. The following is an example of the traditional outline format:

I. Major element
   A. Subheading, significant part of
       subheading idea
      1. Ideas which develop the sub heading
      2. More ideas
          a. details and facts which support an idea

The outline can be as detailed as you need it to be. Refer to the brainstorming sheet to make sure you include all relevant points. Grouping related ideas allows you to readily plug the product of your brainstorm into the outline. Writing the paper will then grow naturally out of the outline that you have created.

The First Draft

You have successfully hurdled the first two major obstacles. You brainstormed inventive ideas; you slam-dunked a solid outline. Saddle the horses, it's time to write.

Or is it? I find that now is a good time to take a mental break. The mind can only sustain an intense focus for so long before it needs recharging. Get physical! Go for a run, play some basketball, do whatever it takes to burn off some energy. Get relaxed! Take a hot shower or soak in a hot tub. Indulge yourself in some let-down time. Have some laughs! Watch a funny movie or read a humorous book (Dilbert, Dave Barry, and The Far Side are personal favorites). Working up a sweat, winding down, and having some fun can be planned into the schedule as rewards for the hard work you've done. The physical/mental/social break allows you to rejuvenate and power up for returning to a high level of focus when you write your first draft. It is just as essential a component of the creative process as any other part of getting ready to write. Having some mental space away from your paper energizes your ability to make last-minute changes before starting to write the first draft.

Okay, now you are ready to jump on that horse and ride. Tape the outline up where it is readily visible and assemble your reference cards (discussed in Power Techniques). All you have to do is follow your outline.

There are lots of little tips and tricks to help you make your paper good reading. One is to use a quotation, which you can hopefully find on your reference card; it can add dimension and emphasis to your paper. This is especially effective when the original author has an understandable or memorable way of making a point.

Here are some more ideas to heighten the creative process.

48

Top Six Tips for Writing Creatively

1. Put your proofreading instincts on hold. Don't bother to make corrections to spelling or grammar at this point. You can do that later, either on your own or using the functions of the computer. When you stop to make minor changes that can easily be done later, you take the chance of losing your train of thought and compromising the flow of your writing.

2. If you get stuck for the right word, put in a word that is near to what you want to say, then use the thesaurus feature on your word processing program. The right word may just emerge from this; certainly it will open up all sorts of other possibilities.

3. If you can't remember a name, a date, or a statistic, mark your place with a symbol (###) to call you attention to it when you come back to revise and polish your work.

4. Sometimes the words just don't flow and you can't seem to say what you want, how you want. Relax your shoulders. Close your eyes. Take a deep breath. Now try saying what you want to say, but just in your mind. Play with it in your mind till it sounds right to you. Repeat what you now want to write once or twice before opening your eyes and putting the words down. By doing this, you eliminated the mental effort (however small) needed to type the words. You briefly reduced external stimuli to increase mental focus and unleash creativity.

5. Eliminate distractions. Kill the ringer on the phone and let the answering machine field your calls. Have whatever food and drink you require at hand before you start. Put a "Do Not Disturb" sign on the door and shut it to the outside world.

49

6. Plan to write for about an hour before taking a brief break. Remember, the mind can sustain intensity for only so long before efficiency drops off. If you find that you are struggling to keep focused before the hour is up, take a physical inventory. Are you becoming tense? Do you need a short break to regain your focus? You'll find your own rhythm, but regardless of how often you take breaks, keep them short so that when you do get back to work, you'll be able to jump back into the flow with ease.

Putting On the Polish: The Revision

You've written your first draft; now it's time to smooth out the rough edges.

Structure and content revision take place at this level. In the first reading, check to see that the paper has a logical flow. The points should be made in such a way that someone reading the paper for the first time could easily make an outline from its content. Ask yourself: Do facts, ideas, and conclusions follow logically from one to another? If they don't, you must rework the paper until they do.

The next important task of revision is to check your facts. Your reference cards are a huge asset in helping you confirm that you've presented correct factual support for your assertions. Also evaluate whether you have provided references for all that you need to. A good rule of thumb is what I call the "Prove It Test." If a fact cannot stand on its own as being universally recognized as true, it probably needs to be referenced. This will encompass any very specific data, any quotations, any piece of information that provides special support for your paper. When you reference a fact in the body of your paper, you must list the source in the reference list at the end of your paper. This information is essential to identifying and retrieving information about your sources.

The next level of revision is the evaluation of style and form. The grammar check on the word processing program can catch many of the errors in style and form, and the spell check will correct most spelling errors. However, despite their sophistication, these programs are imperfect and can still miss important details. You must take charge of making sure all is correct.

The following is a useful list to help you identify and correct common mistakes.

Top Seven Common Style and Form Mistakes

1 Switching tense. Pay strict attention to the tense in which you write. If you are writing about an event in the past, use the past tense. Your references will always be referred to in the present tense. Be especially careful to use the same tense consistently when referring to the same piece of information.

2. Choosing the wrong pronoun. It is rarely appropriate
    to use pronouns in the first person ("I," "we," "us") or
    second person ("you") in a scholarly work. Use "it,"
    "they," and other third-person pronouns, but be clear
    as to whom "it" and "they" refer.

3. Writing poorly constructed sentences. Are your
    sentences complete, meaning that they contain a
    subject and a verb? Are the sentences longer than
    you can say in one small breath? A very skilled writer
    once told me to read Hemingway, for he was a master
    of saying a great deal with an economy of words. Try
    saying it simply, but completely.

4. Using long, pedantic, or little known words. Resist
    the temptation to put in a two-dollar word where a
    fifty-cent word will do. When you use a vocabulary
    that is familiar, you make it easy for the reader to
    understand your point. Keep it simple and direct.

51

5. Assuming a reader's knowledge. While you may
    become acquainted with some specialized terms from
    doing your reading, by listening to lectures, and in
    developing your paper, assume that your reader does
    not have your knowledge base. Define specialized
    terms in all cases and general terms when they are
    used in a unique way.

6. Trying to be funny. A line from the movie Men in
    Black comes to mind: "Madam, we at the FBI are not
    issued a sense of humor that I know of." As tempting
    as going for the laugh might be, scrap the notion of
    using humor in your scholarly works. You might miss
    the mark and it will bring down the tone of
    your paper.

7. Playing to the wrong audience. For whom you are
    writing should be one of the very first questions you
    ask yourself when writing a paper. Your aim is to

communicate your ideas clearly and directly to other professionals. You are engaged in formal writing, which informs rather than entertains. Although this style of writing is very different from creative writing, your creativity is still important in the entire process.

The transition from creative to formal writing is one of the most difficult for new writers to make. As you probably have guessed, this book is not written in the formal style.

More Polish

The first revision is finished. It's time to get physical, get relaxed, and have some laughs again. When you focus intensely on writing a paper, you can lose your perspective. You become too close to the work to see where further improvement could be made. Print out a hard copy and put the draft away for a day or two. You want to give your brain time to recharge, so that you will be able to approach the paper with fresh eyes. Revision, like writing, is a process.

When you next pick up the paper, you will be looking to brighten it up, to make it shine. Read the paper aloud. While this may sound silly, you will be surprised how many problems are discovered when you listen to the words. If it's awkward to say, then it's awkwardly written. All the problems with grammar, transitions, and sentence structure will jump out at you. Use a highlighter to mark the rough spots and keep reading.

By this time, you have developed what could almost be called a relationship with your paper. You have brought it into the world and spent a lot of time and effort nurturing it along, much like a parent. Now it's time for you to give your baby over to the hands—or rather, eyes and mind—of others. Let someone you trust, and whose opinion you value, read and critique your paper. Fresh eyes will see things that you cannot. Include copy of the "Top Seven Common Style and Form Mistakes" and ask this person to evaluate the paper using those criteria. Give permission to be blunt and your assurance that your feelings will not be hurt if he or she is critical of your work. As a writer, you need to develop a thick skin to deal with sharp criticism of your developing skill.

Another benefit grows out of this whole process. Not only do you become more skilled as a writer, but also someone who can edit and critique pieces of work. You are training your mind in critical analysis of information. Acquiring this skill is as important an outcome of education as developing a fund of knowledge. A case in point which demonstrates this can be found in the want ads. Many jobs list a level of degree as a criterion for a job, rather than a specific major. Employers want people with the ability to think, and that skill is assumed for those who have completed a process of formal education.

53

Learning to write well is an integral part of training your mind to think. Like most things in life, becoming good at it requires practice. The more you write, the easier it will become; the more often you can apply advice from others who have mastered this skill, the more polished and professional your writing will be. And as you push yourself toward becoming a good writer and critical thinker, remember that these skills will help you in all areas of life.

Notes

Self Care: Keeping the Mind and Body Well Tuned

"Those who think they have not time for bodily exercise will sooner or later have to find time for illness."

-Edward Stanley,

"The Conduct of Life" Address to Liverpoole College, December 1873.

The mind and the body share a powerful relationship. The mind is the directing force in the use of the body; and the health and well-being of the body influences the mind's ability to function.

Physical fatigue decreases mental acuity, hampering the mind's ability to think clearly and to filter stimuli from the environment. Think of the driver with a car's whose steering keeps pulling to one side. The driver has to expend so much effort and concentration on just keeping the car on the road that his attention is diverted from other important aspects of driving, such as noticing traffic signs and watching for oncoming cars. It's only a matter of time until an accident occurs.

The student who is physically tired suffers all sorts of obstacles to studying. It becomes difficult to concentrate. The need to reread material increases. Writing ceases to flow easily. Task persistence is reduced. Physical fatigue leaves us less motivated to gear up for the mental effort and demand of performing the tasks that school requires. We find ways to avoid getting started doing our work. The few minutes indulgence we allow ourselves before we hit the books draws out and becomes an hour. We find ourselves distracted easily.

When we finally do get started, our tiredness saps our creativity. Higher mental processes either shut down or function so poorly that it becomes a struggle to create. Many artists and writers purposely plan their creative work for the morning, since this is when they are most rested.

The way to manage physical and mental fatigue is simply to get adequate rest. Of course, the pressure of school can push you to study long after you have become tired. You have deadlines to meet, you are afraid you don't know the material as well as you should, you feel overwhelmed and afraid you can't get it all done. However, there comes a point when the cost of continuing to study exceeds the benefits. There is no point in sacrificing your rest when you can't use that time for optimum study.

The answer is to study at times when you feel you can do so most effectively. Retention of information depends more on the quality rather then the quantity of study. Don't expect to retain material well when you're really beat. It just won't happen. I suggest using the early hours of the day for strenuous mental activity, such as studying, and saving the less demanding tasks, those that put less of a demand on your ability to think, for the end of the day. And know when to say "that's enough for one day" and get some rest.

Sleep

Sleep is the body's way of recharging its batteries. How much sleep is necessary to be truly rested? The amount will vary during your lifetime, depending on your age, physical and mental output, diet, exercise, and other factors. Most people will need about eight hours of sleep; this is a median amount. Some individuals feel fully rested after five to six hours; others need nine or more hours. There are researchers who suggest that the minimum is four to five hours in a twenty-four hour period; when we fall below that, task performance suffers greatly. The right amount of sleep for you is that which leaves you feeling fully alert throughout the course of the day.

Our change in lifestyle over the last few decades has altered our sleep. At the turn of the century, most people got on average nine hours of sleep, which coincided loosely with the hours of daylight and nighttime. Sleepiness is influenced by circadian rhythms which are light mediated, and in the past, when there were fewer options for entertainment, people went to bed when it got dark. Today we compress more into our everyday life. We often participate in activities well into the nighttime. And at the end of a long day, we often watch television, which competes with sleep time.

People in North America and Japan work more hours than people anywhere else in the world. Americans are regularly sleepy at some time during the day, the combination of too much work and not enough sleep. As days and weeks of this lifestyle wear on, sleep deprivation becomes cumulative. Researchers describe this process as "sleep debt." It's a debt that needs to be paid in full; but you don't necessarily have to make up for every hour of sleep lost. Most people will catch up if they can allow themselves two consecutive nights where they sleep as much as they want. For night-shift workers, the problem is worse. Working the night shift distorts the person's circadian rhythm. Yet many students work night shifts to accommodate their schedules at school, and for some students it can allow them to have large blocks of time to study. But they pay a price for maintaining this kind of schedule, as their recovery time is far longer. It may be three to four days before full daytime alertness and mental acuity is achieved, and that recovery period may be filled with frequent waking. The student who must work nights should group work shifts and days off as much as possible. This limits the number of times you have to turn around your awake-sleep pattern.

If you choose—or are required—to work night shifts, do so on a part-time basis, if at all possible. This allows more time to catch up on sleep and "pay off" your sleep debt. Work that requires you to be mentally clear, such as studying, is best put off until the time when you have recovered from working nights.

Most of us experience difficulty in sleeping from time to time, but for many people sleep is a chronic problem. Sleep disturbance is a hallmark of depression or its less severe form, dysthymia. For the depressed person, sleep patterns are characterized by difficulty falling asleep, too few hours of sleep, and early morning waking. If you find yourself in a low mood on an ongoing basis, then it is time to think about depression or dysthymia as a possible cause. These are treatable problems; make an appointment with a trained clinician to get proper treatment.

What about those people who aren't depressed, but still have a problem sleeping? Behaviors can inadvertently interfere with the ability to sleep, and fairly minor changes in lifestyle can make enormous differences. Consider the following:

Top Ten List of Ways to Improve Your Sleep

1. Avoid caffeine, nicotine, and alcohol before going to bed. Caffeine is a very active drug which stimulates the central nervous system for up to seven hours. It is a leading culprit in causing sleeplessness (more on this later). Nicotine is also a stimulant and can interfere

with sleep. Alcohol, while initially sedating, is a central nervous system irritant and can lead to fragmented sleep.

2. No naps! You want to be tired at bedtime. Naps can rest your body but don't do the job for your brain. A nap usually does not provide full-cycle sleep (including dream and deep-sleep intervals) which takes an average of ninety minutes. We need full-cycle sleep to feel fully rested. If you absolutely can't make it through the course of the day without a nap, lie down for no more than one hour and do this before three in the afternoon.

   There are some people who find they can take a quick catnap—about twenty to thirty minutes—and come away refreshed. One of our country's great minds, Thomas Edison, often took catnaps. However, for the majority of people, naps interfere with continuous night-time sleep, disrupting sleep patterns and doing more harm than good.

3. No exercise for at least ninety minutes before bed time. Regular exercise will definitely help you sleep better. The effects of exercise on sleep happen within a few days of starting to exercise. Even twenty minutes of some kind of exercise per day can produce remarkable effects on sleep. However, exercise raises metabolism and body temperature, both of which can interfere with sleep, so you don't want to do anything too taxing close to bedtime.

4. Have a light snack before bedtime. A heavy meal before bedtime can leave you feeling like a beached whale, definitely not the way to help yourself fall asleep. Dairy products and turkey both contain L-tryptophan, an amino acid that acts as a natural sleep inducer.

5. Only use your bed for sleeping and sex. We make associations to physical space, so we don't want to associate our bed with work. The same goes for television; when you get in bed, don't turn on the TV. You want your body to know that when you get into bed, it is time to sleep. Sex generally leaves people feeling very relaxed, which is a natural precursor to rest and a great association to have before going to sleep.

6. Sleep only when you're sleepy. Time spent struggling to fall asleep in bed builds a subtle association that your bed is a difficult place to fall asleep. You might notice that after spending hours trying to fall asleep in bed, you can readily fall asleep on the couch. The negative association linked with the difficulty in falling asleep in bed is at work here.

7. If you can't fall asleep in twenty minutes, get out of bed and engage in some activity with low mental stimulation until you feel sleepy. Don't turn on the television. It's too easy to get engaged in watching TV, even the really bad TV which often airs late at night. Read something boring, but don't expose yourself to bright light. Light signals the brain that it is time to turn off production of melatonin in the brain, and this tells our bodies that it's time to wake up.

8. Get up and go to bed at the same time each day. A regular rhythm for your sleep cycle is very helpful in maintaining good sleep. Of course, you probably can't do this every day, given that some social activities may keep you out late. If you keep regular hours on most days, however, your body will fall into a natural rhythm.

9. Take a hot bath ninety minutes before you want to go to bed. A hot bath can be very relaxing, but timing is

60

important. A hot bath raises the body's core temperature; when the body cools down, it is the drop in body temperature that cues the body to go to sleep.

10. Create the optimum sleep environment. A cool room and warm blankets is the desired mix. Just like Goldilocks, too hot or too cold interferes with falling asleep. Use sound to mask other sounds in the environment; a fan to create "white noise" or recordings of sounds from nature can be very helpful. Since light can keep you from falling asleep and or staying asleep, dark shades help decrease morning light. If you sleep with a partner who reads in bed, use blinders to cut the light out.

Turning the Mind Off at the End of the Day

We all experience it. We have those days when we find ourselves preoccupied with the events of the day. Our bodies and indeed our minds are tired, but we just can't turn off our thinking process. We toss and turn, searching in vain for a comfortable position; try as we might, we keep thinking and worrying about all sorts of things. It would be one thing if the thoughts were productive. But this kind of stewing and fretting is not. We tend to fall into a pattern of thought where we ruminate, chewing on the same thoughts over and over without progress or resolution.

These periods where we can't turn our brains off are much like a state of anxiety, which whether produced by specific or nonspecific stresses can elicit strong emotions. Whenever you find yourself falling into these thought patterns, you want to take control and direct the course of your thoughts away from this unproductive type of preoccupation. You can use the strong mind-body connection to move you away from restless to relaxed by changing your response to the stresses of the day; to do this, you must change the stimulus to which you are responding. By far the easiest way to bring this about is by use of a skill called "guided imagery."

When you use guided imagery, you allow your mind to guide itself on a journey, one that consists of pleasant images. They can be real or imagined, vivid or tranquil, but they must ease rather than excite or stress. And because of the connection between mind and body, where the mind goes, the body follows.

You may need some direction to acquire this skill, and a good place to start is with a tape. Many health food stores will carry various relaxation tapes on which a narrator guides you on a journey of imagery. These are temporary training tools, giving you the experience of the mind purposely following a guided path to peaceful images and places. However, the mind is an amazingly industrious organ. More often than not, it will want to go back to being active, and it may slip into a more real-time, evaluative mode. It's not uncommon for people to notice small imperfections in the tape, then start anticipating them on subsequent playings, which of course distracts them from the guided journey. Still, the tapes give you an initial experience in creating journeys; once indoctrinated, you can create your own. Self-created imagery is more flexible and can be infinitely more variable by allowing you to introduce your own unique fantasies into the imagery.

Another tool for guided imagery is the use of background sounds. There are many CDs and tapes available with a variety of natural sounds, such as those found in a rain forest or on a beach, and they can be found everywhere from small specialty stores to the discount megamarts. You want the images you create to match the background sound you choose, so don't imagine a walk in the woods if the background sounds convey a pounding surf.

The purpose of using background sound is to stimulate our sensory channels in a highly directed manner. We inundate our auditory sense with sounds that relax rather than interrupt our ability to sleep. Recorded natural sounds are an excellent way of masking other background noises, allowing us to take control of not only our external environment but our internal one as well.

To take even more control over your internal environment, borrow a technique from hypnosis. After starting the background sound, fix your gaze on an object just above your normal forward field of vision. If you need glasses to see an object clearly, but you don't want to go to sleep with them on, you can instead just focus on an area of light or shadow. Repeat to yourself the phrase "My eyes feel heavy." The act of looking upward indeed makes your eyes feel heavy, and you enhance that feeling of fatigue in the eyes by the verbal suggestion.

63

Next let's consider the body. Focus on the sensation created by your body's contact with your bed—the weight of your body, the coolness of the sheets, the firmness of the mattress. When your concentration shifts to defining particular physical sensations, this occupies your thoughts filling yet another sensory channel.

You further fill your sensory channel by focusing on your breathing. Breathe in to a slow count of three and hold your breath for just a moment before exhaling. As you exhale, do so to a slow count of three and, again, momentarily hold your breath once you've exhaled. Notice the sense of innercalm during the moment you hold your breath. This technique is called the "quieting breath" and has other applications, particularly in dealing with test anxiety and public speaking.

Given what we've talked about here, let's begin a guided journey of imagery. Keep in mind that the image needs to employ all of the senses. If you are imagining walking on the beach, you should feel the sand, hear the birds and the surf, smell the saltwater, and feel the breeze on our face. You can intensify the latter by using a small fan set on low, blowing in the direction of your face. When you combine the recorded sounds and a small fan to intensify your sensory experience, you effect a profound sense of relaxation. It will actively redirect the course of your thinking and turn off the unproductive ruminating.

Like anything else, the more you practice relaxing and redirecting your thoughts, the better you will become. Self-management of your internal environment is no less a skill than learning how to take tests well.

I mentioned earlier the importance of incorporating all of the senses during the course of the guided imagery. It is also important to pair physical sensations with the elements of the image to cue relaxation. Here is a guided image to suggest ideas and help you get started.

A Walk on the Beach - A Script for Relaxation

You are walking along the beach. It is early in the evening and the sun is low on the horizon. The time of year is mid-August. Heat radiates up from the warm sand mixing with the cool breeze coming off of the ocean. You take off your sandals and feel the warmth of the sand. Your feet sink in slightly as sand surrounds your toes. The smell of the sea fills your nostrils. You taste a residue of salt on your lips from the spray of the surf.

Hear the thunder of the waves as they crash upon the shore. Notice the hiss of the water as it sprints up the flat sand toward your feet. Breathe with the slow rhythm of the waves, becoming aware of feeling more relaxed with each breath. Exhale slowly as the wave recedes from the shore.

64

Look forward to the sand dunes. A fine mist envelops them in the golden light of the setting sun. The mist floats from the water to the shore. Seagulls laugh in the wind that washes the mist toward shore. The mist undulates in soft waves as it caresses the golden dunes. The sea becomes a silvery mirror as shades of violet and scarlet mix with the golden glow of the sun.

Sit down on the side of one of the dunes. Feel the warmth of the sand on your hands as you lean back on the sand. The whoosh of the crashing waves enfolds you. You are surrounded by the smell of the salt air as the cool breeze from the ocean slowly fills your lungs. Your breathing matches the ebb and flow of the waves. Lie farther back, feeling the warmth of the sand caress your back. The sand shapes to your form and you feel relaxed, heavy, perfectly supported. The sun becomes lower, finally disappearing below the horizon. The sky is filled with rich colors of violet, pink, scarlet, and orange. With the sound of each wave you become more deeply relaxed. Your whole body feels warm as you float upon the sand. The seagulls' cries become more distant. Allow yourself to just drift, surrounded by the warmth of the sand and the pleasant song of the ocean.

Food for Thought

What and how we eat profoundly affects both performance and mood, beginning with when we wake up, continuing throughout the day, and even influencing our ability to fall asleep and remain asleep.

The physiology of eating is a product of our hunter-gatherer origins. For example, when we first wake up in the morning, it is common to not feel actively hungry. This is adaptive behavior, since a hunter-gatherer's first task of the day is to find food, and doing so is much easier if the stomach is not growling.

The sensation of hunger is not brought on by an empty stomach but by a lowered level of blood glucose, which activates receptors in the brain that respond by producing the sensation of hunger. After a night's sleep, we are at a low point in our blood glucose level; however, our adaptation to our former hunter-gatherer origins subverts the sensation of hunger, allowing us to find food without that distraction. Because those hunger pangs are suppressed, many people don't make breakfast a priority. They're not hungry, they reason, so why eat? The answer to that question is that breakfast is necessary to bring up the blood sugar to a normal level.

When you eat a well-balanced breakfast, you actively increase cognitive abilities, energy level, and mood. This means incorporating carbohydrates, protein, and fats in your morning meal, which can be as simple as having a bowl of cereal with milk. You want all three types of food because each one is digested at a different rate: carbohydrates break down first, protein next, and fats digest the slowest. When you combine these food groups, you provide yourself with energy that nourishes you throughout the day.

Food is very reinforcing. The sensation of something in your stomach and the warmth it generates enhance a sense of well-being and comfort. Many people make the mistake of starting their day with just a cup of hot coffee or tea. Although this creates the sensation of fullness and warmth in the stomach, it does nothing to sustain metabolism. Carbohydrates in particular provide a good source of energy as they are time-release foods. Many runners and other athletes "carb load" the night before they run or play. Carbohydrates enter the system quickly and convert to glycogen, which the body then stores for later use when energy demand is high. You will find carbohydrates in plant foods such as cereals, grains, and fruits; in fact, the only source of animal carbohydrates is lactose in milk.

Now let's look at how we eat for the rest of the day. As a hunter-gatherer species, we have been programmed to be opportunistic feeders. If the early human came upon something to eat, they ate at least a portion of it immediately. This saved on having to store and carry food. As a result, our prehistoric ancestors were eating throughout the course of the day.

Our current habit of consuming three meals a day is more a social custom rather than a good fit for our physiology. In our recent past, conventional thought dictated a big breakfast, lunch, and dinner. Now we know that eating strategically means consuming five to six small meals per day. We sustain our metabolism better by eating a moderate breakfast, a midmorning snack, a small lunch, an afternoon snack, a moderate dinner, and a bedtime snack. Dinner should not be our biggest meal, as it often is, but enough to sustain us through the four to five hours afterward in which we may be engaged in mental work. Like our hunter-gatherer ancestors, our most effective way of feeding our bodies is to graze all day long, which keeps our blood sugar from dropping and sustains our energy throughout the day.

Eating strategically involves more than just the timing of meals and snacks. Foods can either activate and energize or calm and relax, depending on the amino acid that they release. If you have a midafternoon presentation, you will want to be energized and functioning at peak activation. Time for protein. Protein releases the amino acid tyrosine, the precursor of two major hormones, dopamine and norepinephrine. While the names of the hormones are not important, their effect is. They activate the person.

The trail snack GORP (so named for its "gobs of raisins and peanuts") provides a good example of a pick-me-up snack. Actually GORP can consist of any combination of nuts, dried fruits, and small pieces of chocolate or carob, providing a mix of food groups doing different things. The chocolate, with its high glucose content, enters the system rapidly for immediate energy. The nuts are a good source of protein and sustained-release calories. The fruit, with its fructose content, also gives a quick energy boost, but because of its cellulose structure, digestion takes longer. Often we don't get enough fruit and vegetables in our diet, particularly when we are on the run. A couple of handfuls of GORP can be a delicious and quick way to incorporate fruit into our diet. There are also many commercially marketed energy bars that combine many of the same ingredients as GORP.

Eating for sleep requires a different strategy. A starting point is becoming aware of your caffeine intake. Caffeine is a central nervous stimulator. Its effect can last in the neighborhood of seven hours. For those people sensitive to caffeine, a small amount may have significant effects; others may build a tolerance to it, just as can be done with any drug.

68

The best policy is to set a caffeine cut-off time in the late afternoon. And be aware of hidden sources of caffeine; it lurks in an assortment of beverages, not just the colas.

The following relative caffeine contents are published by the National Soft Drink Association and are according to Bunker and McWilliams in the J. AM. Diet. 74:28-32, 1979.

Caffeine Contents Product	mg.
Jolt	71.2
Mountain Dew	55
Kick Citrus	54
Tab	46.8
Coca-Cola (Diet and Reg.)	45.6

Shasta Cola	44.4
Shasta Cherry Cola	44.4
Dr. Pepper	39.6
Pepsi Cola	37.2
Diet Pepsi	35.4
RC Cola	36
Canada Dry Cola	30
Canada Dry Diet Cola	1.2
7 Up	0
Drip coffee	115-175
Espresso (1.5-2 oz.)	100
Tea, brewed, imported	60
Tea, brewed, U.S.	40
Decaf	2 - 4
Chocolate-baking 1 oz.	25
Chocolate-semi-sweet, baker's 1 oz.	13
Chocolate chips	13 - 15
Chocolate bar, milk	30
Chocolate bar, Cadbury 1 oz.	15
Jello Chocolate Fudge Mousse	12
Chocolate powder mix, 3 Tbs.	8
Cold relief tablet	30 (avg.)

The snack you choose for bedtime should not be glucose dense, meaning high in sugar content. Cake with lots of frosting or candy bars are examples of high-sugar snacks that will cause a rapid surge in your blood sugar as they speed into your system. The entry of glucose is rapid indeed. Glucose is given to diabetics as an intervention for low blood sugar because it can quickly enter the system. The rapid surge in blood sugar then activates the body's production of insulin.

Sometimes hunger can wake us up during the middle of the night despite the adaptive suppression of hunger we experience after waking from a normal sleep cycle. A snack containing carbohydrates are ideal for sustaining us through the night. They enter into the system fairly rapidly and store glycogen for later use, suppressing late-night hunger pangs.

The best bedtime snacks are those foods high in L-tryptophan. This amino acid has the unique property of linking with our natural circadian rhythm and causing us to feel sleepy at night when we're ready for sleep. Milk products and turkey both have adequate amounts of L-tryptophan. An ideal bedtime snack consists of half a turkey sandwich and a glass of milk, which adds value in three ways: It provides nutrition, creates a sense of warmth and a light fullness in the stomach, and contributes the effective L-tryptophan to the system. These combine to comfort and lull you to sleep.

70

Alcohol produces a sedative action and may induce people to feel sleepy. However, it also irritates the central nervous system. That awful hangover that comes from too much imbibing is the central nervous system suffering irritation caused by alcohol. While you may find alcohol in moderation to be helpful in relaxing you prior to sleep, try a comparison with milk products—one night using alcohol to help you sleep, the next night trying a glass of milk or some yogurt. You may find yourself surprised at the effectiveness of dairy products when compared to alcohol.

Invest in Exercise

Most of us can find a hundred and one reasons not to exercise, yet its benefits are numerous. When we work under highly demanding conditions, exercise can reduce stress. It keeps are bodies agile, strong, and healthy. And it helps us think.

Exercise has a way of cleaning out the mental cobwebs and improving the thinking processes on a number of different levels. Having some vigorous exercise prior to settling down for an extended period of study will make you feel more physically relaxed and increase your alertness, which combine to help you intensely focus on your work. Exercise can make us feel better psychologically as well. When we work at a high level of intensity, we can often feel like our life is running us rather than we are running our life. What little energy we have left after we fulfill the demands of school and work we want to give to the significant people in our life. But to fill another's cup, our own well needs to have something in it. Exercise can be a way in which we give something back to ourselves. Everyone needs a means of emotional and physical release, and exercise can provide that.

I like to plan at least one session per week where I participate in vigorous exercise. I think of it as a reward for working at a high level of performance. By giving myself a regular release to the stress and tension created by a busy, high-demand lifestyle, I become more able to tolerate continued stress. And exercise increases the temporary release of hormones called endorphins, which allow us to feel a greater sense of well-being and energy.

Speaking of energy, everyone knows that exercise takes energy—but it also creates it. When we increase our cardiovascular health, our hearts pump more blood, which rejuvenates every facet of our body. Lungs increase in their capacity. Muscle and joint flexibility and strength increase. We become more vigorous and find that we actually have more energy and stamina as a result.

When is the best time to exercise? Whenever you can. We all have times during our day when we feel more energetic than others. The trick is to find a good time to fit it in. If you find yourself frequently skipping the time set aside to exercise, look at switching the time of day.

Motivation to exercise can be hard to summon up. You can remove a barrier to that motivation by exercising when it's convenient.

Try to find a number of different ways to exercise. Performing the same exercises and following the same routine can make exercising seem dull and regimented. We all need variety; our minds crave novelty and the stimulation created by doing different things. Nothing saps the life out of exercising like boredom, so be careful not to fall into that trap.

Exercise Is Where You Find It

Life has many hidden opportunities for exercise. For example, parking on most campuses is difficult at best and expensive to boot. Why not park away from campus and walk in? This is a great way to create an opportunity to exercise; it will energize you as you start your academic day and help you wind down afterwards.

Whenever possible, take the stairs instead of the elevator or escalator. Don't waste your money paying for the use of a stair-stepper at a health club; a long flight of steps works just as well and is free.

How many students carry around a book bag? Most everyone, filled with books that weigh quite a bit. How about doing ten to twelve reps with a book bag instead of a barbell? Lifting weight is lifting weight, be it a book bag or a barbell. And you can do this when you're stuck waiting somewhere instead of trying to fit a trip to the gym into your already packed schedule.

Getting Started

The U.S. Surgeon General released a report in 1996 that documented the importance of physical activity and exercise. How much to exercise and for how long has been debated for years. What became clear from the Surgeon General's report, however, is that no matter what kind of exercise program you start, if you haven't been exercising, a slow beginning followed by a gradual increase to greater duration and intensity over a period of time is important.

As a seasoned weight lifter and regular in the gym, I have seen a particular scenario repeated over and over again. New members will come into the weight room and immediately try to lift more weight than they should, simply because others in the gym are lifting that much. All they get is a lot of pain from sore muscles, which then often deters them from continuing a sustained program.

Many college and university gyms and most private gyms will give assistance in developing an exercise program. Take advantage of the knowledge and expertise they offer you. Even the most experienced and fit person in the gym had to start somewhere. It's important for you to begin at your level, not at someone else's.

73

Who is at risk for starting an exercise program? Most people, if they start slowly and build up in duration and intensity, will be just fine. Men over age forty and women over age fifty who have been inactive, as well as people who are at high risk for cardiovascular disease, should consult their doctor before getting started. The National Institute of Health identified physical inactivity as a major public health problem. Many health problems would be better controlled, even alleviated or prevented, by the simple act of getting regular exercise. When you do so, you improve your mental acuity, your energy, and your endurance, all which you carry throughout your day.

The important thing is to get started!

Notes

Putting Yourself to the Test

"I believe that testing of the students achievement in order to see if he meets some criterion held by the teacher is directly contrary to the implication of therapy for significant learning".

-Carl Rogers

Evaluation of the student's mastery of a course's information is a fact of academic life. Instructors assess a student's proficiency in a number of ways: presentations, papers, participation in class discussion and, of course, formal testing. While a grade is an important measure of a student's mastery, too often it becomes a goal unto itself, overshadowing the original goal of personal mastery of the information. If a student approaches learning from the perspective of wanting to understand, use, and truly master the information a teacher has to give, then positive measures of evaluation naturally follow.

Focusing only on getting a good grade can be a source of great pressure on the student, detracting from the academic experience of this unique time of growth, and the mind is pushed beyond its previous limits. If the goal of education is knowledge rather than grades, however, the focus shifts to a more positive motivation, and the knowledge gained bespeaks a personal mastery of the information studied. Grades are but a reflection of that mastery.

Grades are nevertheless important. Corporations often use transcripts as a measure of a candidate's inherent abilities. Class standing has a direct correlation to future income in a number of different fields. Access to future education is often determined by a grade point average.

The higher one goes in education, the more competition there will be among students for access to that education and entry into those high-demand programs will depend on previous academic success. So, doing well in school is always desirable. But the skills needed to glean the most out of education are the same skills used to successfully navigate in the realm of formal evaluation. When you demand a high level of mastery for your learning, excellent grades are a natural outcome of your mastery.

76

Building a Foundation

Demand as much from yourself as you demand from your professor. When I went to school I had a professor who was regarded as one of the national leaders in the field of alcohol studies, and he wrote an excellent book on the subject. Unfortunately, when he lectured in class, all he did was regurgitate his book.

Since I was paying for my education myself, I decided to figure out just what it cost for me to be in his class. (This is an interesting exercise and a big help if you are considering whether one of your classes might be expendable.) At this small, private university, I was paying over $40 for each ninety minutes of class time. For that kind of money I wanted more than what I could get on my own by reading the book—especially when I had an opportunity to learn directly from a nationally regarded expert.

When I confronted the professor, I had to come to grips with my part of the relationship. If I was going to demand more from my instructor, I had to be ready to demand more from myself. For every student, that starts with class time.

When you strive for excellence, you need to make the most of your classroom time. Think of it as an opportunity. To take advantage of any opportunity, you must be adequately prepared. Always complete your assigned reading prior to coming to class. If you don't, and you rely on hearing material "cold," you may find yourself lost. You want your classroom time to be a time of active learning. When you come prepared, what you learned from your reading is reinforced and pushed to a higher level by the discussion in class.

Develop a "heads up" attitude about participating in class. Get to class on time. Return from breaks on time. In nursing school, I had an instructor who closed and locked the door when break time was over. If you didn't quite make it back in time, too bad—you lost out. What this instructor demanded was the same level of professionalism about school that is demanded in the working world. The habits and attitudes you develop while in school directly translate to the same habits and attitudes you will need to excel in your career.

Overcome "first row-itis." Whenever there are plenty of seats for students, the first row in a classroom will often remain vacant. But notice where the best students tend to sit—nearest the instructor. Those who aren't doing as well are found in the back half of the classroom. You want to be one of those students fighting for a seat in the front! Where else are you going to be able to see and hear things best?

The front row is the least distracting place to sit, particularly if it is a mega-class with five hundred to a

77

thousand students. And when you sit in the front, you stay more alert. Because you have a sense of direct contact with your instructor, you are less likely to let your thoughts drift. You become an active listener, which makes it easier to pull out the truly key information. This focused concentration has the effect of blotting out the distractions in the room.

In the mega-class scenario, sitting in the front will give you other advantages. The instructor in a mega-class can only make eye contact with those people sitting in the front; the rest of the class becomes an impersonal sea of faces. When you sit in the front, the professor is more likely to know your name and view you on a more personal level. You also convey that you are there to learn, to take an active role in the class, not just to get through.

78

In smaller classes and study groups, discussion becomes the focal point. Be prepared to actively engage in discussion, because this is where you will develop a higher level of understanding and mastery. Discussion acts as a catalyst in developing new and different perspectives on a subject and will give you the opportunity to develop critical thinking skills. The intellectual stimulation that discussion provokes can be one of the best rewards of the academic experience. Passion and ideas often mix, leaving you contemplating course material long after the class has ended. Wherever you can achieve that level and type of stimulation, memory and subsequent recall for exams become much easier.

Hitting the Books

The sheer volume of some textbooks can leave you feeling buried before you even open them up. To keep from being overwhelmed, remember that the task of the student is not to read every word, but to separate the essence of the core material.

Chapter 6 - Putting Yourself to the Test

Core material is what your instructor will use to build an exam. Core material from the hard sciences may be largely fact- and formula-based. High-fact volume requires repetition to learn and is ideally suited to a flash-card format for repeated reviews of material. Core material from the humanities can include concepts, theories, and people and events of note. This information can be adapted to a flash card strategy too. In fact, many different kinds of material can be readily absorbed using the repetition sequence of flash cards.

When you first open a textbook, examine its layout. Many books are formatted to assist you in pulling out the core material. If your text has a chapter outline, the essence of the core material is served to you on a platter. Start by making flash cards with each heading title. Arrange them in the sequential order of the chapter outline. These are the guideposts of the reading, telling you what to expect as you journey through the chapter.

As you begin your reading, notice how the sections start with a main idea or concept. What follows supports the main idea—meaning the "what," "why," and "how" which build the case for the significance of the concept. On your flash card, state the essential facts or information about the basic concept. You can then skim the rest of the section for supporting data, allowing you to cover a lot of reading material in a short amount of time.

Highlighting can help this process. However, curb the urge to highlight more than you need to, as that will diminish its usefulness. For highlighting to be effective, it must be used just to mark the "highlights." Take the same approach as you would to making a flash card. The basic concept, and its support information, are all that should be highlighted, which usually is 10 percent or less of the material. You may want to experiment with highlighting before making flash cards. Because it is quicker to highlight than to write something down, you may find this to be a more efficient way for you to move through the reading and develop your review cards.

Books that don't have a chapter outline are a bit more difficult, but can be approached in essentially the same way. As you begin each chapter, take a few minutes to go through and write down the section headings. These become the road map for the chapter. Headings separate out the various clusters of information, while remaining within an overall organization. And you can use them to title the information on your flash cards. For sections that have multiple concepts, principles, people, or events, titles are a way of grouping related information.

Construction of Memory

Marketing theory tells us that we need at least seven repetitions to remember a name or a fact. Large corporations spend vast amounts of their advertising budget to bombard us with information about their products over and over and over again. We retain irrelevant information—for example, an inane advertising jingle—because we have heard them so many times.

Ever wonder why a fourteen-year-old can have a near-photographic memory for the statistics of a player on his favorite team, yet consistently forget to take out the garbage? Unlike remembering to take out the garbage, recall of team statistics develops from a wish to know, a desire to possess that information. A variety of memory strategies may be employed to recall information, but interest is what motivates a person to invest time in developing recall of information.

The kid who repeatedly goes through his sports cards, reading the stats over and over again, is using spaced repetition. To really seat information into long-term memory and develop fluid recall, this repetition is an essential element to study.

Chapter 6 - Putting Yourself to the Test

When you study, your first repetition of material comes in making flash cards during your initial reading of the material. This is the first step to analyzing the information. Your analysis groups material into meaningful concepts, relationships, and the supportive facts for the core information from your reading.

Your second pass should occur fairly soon after you complete your reading. First, however, take a short break. Stretch, get your circulation going again, wash your face, enjoy a refreshing drink, and generally clear your head. Now you're ready to have the second pass at the information. After you complete this, you will be ready to actively participate in classroom discussion.

Think of the second pass through the material as digestion. You've ingested the information; now you want to see if it makes sense. Do the supporting facts actually support the concept or principle? If you are learning about a particular a person or event, have you described why and how the person or event is important? You want to illustrate how the information may be relevant, on either a personal or professional level. Your goal is to develop an interest that motivates you to invest in long-term recall.

Here is a case in point. Why would a construction manager need to study basic psychology? The subjects of psychology and construction seem pretty far removed from one another. However, what if a study of psychology could give the construction manager different and effective tools to increase productivity and reliability? What if by applying certain psychological principles, he could do things for and with employees that would make them want to stay with the company and feel invested in the product the company creates? For example, he could use the concept of variable schedule and variable amount reinforcement, which asserts that by giving rewards intermittently and in varying amounts, a certain behavior can be established. This type of reinforcement is extremely powerful and one of the reasons gambling is so addictive. As the construction manager comes to understand how he can use this same principle to help his company—for example awarding bonuses of various amounts on an intermittent basis—he becomes more interested and puts more effort into studying psychology. For the student, particularly in introductory classes, it can be very difficult to find relevance and interest, but these are key elements in anchoring long-term recall.

The third pass may come during class, particularly if the class has discussion as part if its daily format. Bring your flash cards to class. Before information is seated into your long-term memory, flash cards can provide you with a quick reference to facts and concepts that make your contribution to a discussion more powerful. When you reference information from your cards, you make a strong statement to your professor. You are perceived as a person who is not only prepared, but has developed insight about the subject matter. You have identified yourself as a higher-level student.

This third pass during class time is where you start to integrate information. You hear more about what you have covered in the reading and you can draw on the expertise of the instructor to clarify and expound on the written information. If you ask a question in class, it makes an impression on you, and the result is that you will recall the information better over the long term. That level of engagement enhances learning in a very powerful way. However slight, the visceral response you have in publicly asking a question gives a physical anchor to the information. The concepts that you struggle most with are the very things that you want to clarify by questioning, either during or after the class.

You will find that repetitions after the third pass become quicker as the material becomes increasingly

82

familiar. Reviews become a building process, as you continually add more information.

On the day of the exam, leave your cards at home. There is a tendency to want to do just one more review prior to sitting for the exam, but a last-minute review can do more to increase anxiety than help you recall the information. If you have had ten to twenty repetitions of the information, YOU WILL RECALL THE INFORMA-TION! For extremely fact-dense subjects like anatomy, you may find that you need more repetitions to retain the vast quantity of information. The saving grace of high-levels of repetitions is that each time you go through your cards, you pick up speed.

Recall of formulas requires a somewhat different approach to using the tool of repetition. You want to be a little bit more creative. If your text has sample questions at the end of the chapter, by all means, take advantage of them—or make up your own sample questions and use them for practice.

83

In the medical profession, there is a teaching axiom: See one, do one, teach one. The "see one" phase is your first exposure to the information. "Do one" refers to taking the information and applying it to a variety of situations. This may be making up similar math problems to solve to gain experience using a formula. The "teach one" phase is the part that most effectively locks in information in memory.

Teaching is an excellent way to integrate and become adept at using the information. How can you teach someone to use a formula? Become a tutor or present information in a study group. If your level of understanding develops to the point where you can teach others, you fine-tune your own understanding of a subject.

Attack Strategies

Imagine for a moment that you are a professional athlete who must perform tomorrow in a big game. To-night you go out to have a good time, maybe have a few drinks, and don't get to bed until very late. Would you expect to perform your best the next day on such short rest? Of course not!

As a student preparing for an exam, you are no different in this respect from the pro athlete preparing for a game. Your first and best attack strategy is to get enough rest so that you are at your sharpest. Eating well, too, is important as you will have less physical distraction from hunger and get an energy boost from the right foods. And on exam day, come to class a little early. Nothing adds to anxiety like having to rush to a class and jump into an exam.

84

Once you begin taking the test, you want to focus on what exactly each question is asking. Take enough time so that you are sure you know what is being asked. You may want to use a highlighter to help focus on the essence of the question. By being thorough in this ap-proach, you help eliminate the common problem of having to change answers as you review the test. When you take the time to read and understand each question adequately the first time you see it, you save yourself a lot of time and trouble.

Deductive Reasoning and Objective Tests

Objective tests, those that are true-false and the multiple choice, are the norm for larger classes. It is just too time-consuming for the instructor to approach evalu-ation any other way. They are also the easiest type of test to take. Objective tests require recognition rather than synthesis. Recognition of what is familiar is a much easier task than the integration of information required in synthesis. They are also the type of test which requires the simplest strategies to determine the answer to the question.

Look for key words, particularly words that denote an absolute. All, none, every, never, always, nothing—these all indicate an absolute. In most fields of study, there are very few absolutes. "All absolutes are false" is in itself an absolute. A good rule of thumb to remember is that a question framed as an absolute will most likely be false.

One way of tripping up students on a true-false question is to pair a true statement with an incorrect one. When a statement is quickly read, the true part jumps out at the test taker. The false part of the question may involve a lesser-known fact or piece of information. The student, responding to the fact known to be true, is often deceived into making the wrong choice.

Multiple choice questions mix recognition with deductive strategies. Using deductive strategies, you can readily chew through the multiple-choice exam. First read the question. Are you sure you know what it is asking? Next, if a fact that you know to be definitely false is stated, you can cross out every answer that contains that fact. Go ahead and put an "X" through that choice.

The corollary to this is generally true as well. If you recognize a fact stated as true, more than likely it will indicate the correct answer. Using this recognition technique helps you reduce your odds of choosing the incorrect answer.

What if you find yourself reading and rereading a question, either because you may not know the answer or you're just stuck for the moment? There is a danger in overreading. You can interpret more than what is being asked in a question. When this happens, mark the question, either with your highlighter or in some other way, and move on. Don't get bogged down and let anxiety build up by struggling with a particular question. As you move through the test, the answer may be sparked by content from another question. In that case, go back and make your selection. If no thunderbolts of insight strike you, wait till you are done with the rest of the exam before going back.

Essay Questions

Essay questions come in two types: descriptive and analytical. Answering either kind begins—once again—with careful reading of the question. Be sure as to what the question is asking. If it gives directions to address particular facets of the question, then highlight those to make sure that they are included in the essay.

The second step, for both descriptive and analytical essay questions, is to form a brief outline of your response. The descriptive is by far the easiest in this regard. Your response grows directly out of the information on the flash cards you've made. You should be readily able to recall the "why" and the "how" the people and events studied were important, and to explain the impact they had in relation to the course's subject.

Comparing or contrasting pieces of information is a further evolution of the descriptive essay. Again, you will use information from your flash cards to show a connection between two or more items. Your outline readily enables you to pick out similarities and differences.

The analytical essay question requires synthesis of facts. The instructor may have you defend a particular point of view rather then let you choose which side of an issue you would like to argue. Whether you are given a predetermined point of view or are allowed to choose your own, you must construct a logical argument by presenting facts which inevitably lead to your conclusion. Here an outline is indispensable, as it is during the formation of an outline that your logic is formed. You save time and are more efficient and effective in presenting your argument when you first construct a short outline instead of fleshing out your thoughts as you write the essay. The outline lets you build simple cause-and-effect relationships; you then have the opportunity to expound on them when you write the essay.

If you have been an active participant in classroom discussion, the experience will come in handy when responding to this type of question. Synthesis of ideas is the natural outcome of discussion, and this process will come to you naturally if you have practiced it in the classroom setting. Again, a brief outline will help you formulate your thoughts and stay focused.

Essay questions should have a common format. The essay must begin with a paragraph that defines the problem, suggests a comparison or contrast, or explains a position the instructor has asked you to write about. While this paragraph may be completed in one or two sentences, it is really the overview of the essay.

The body of the essay contains the supporting facts for what you have been asked to write about. The question will tell you what you must accomplish in the body of the essay, whether it is a listing, a comparison or contrast, an analysis, or just a description.

Each type of essay question should have a brief summary of the importance of an issue or the conclusions you have drawn from your argument. Merely presenting ideas is not enough; you must show that you understand the significance of what you are writing about. The ending is where you describe the importance, impact, or relevance, or state your conclusions about your subject. This draws your essay to a natural close.

Test Anxiety

You arrive on time for the mid-term and find your seat. Suddenly, you become aware that your hands are moist and your pulse is racing. As you wait for the test papers to be handed out, your anxiety grows. You attempt to recall simple facts from your pretest studying and draw a complete blank on things you clearly know. Negative thoughts begin to creep in until you are truly catatonic. "I am going to fail," you tell yourself. The negative emotional thoughts become increasingly irrational and destructive. You think, "Everyone is going to know that I am a failure." When you finally get the test paper and you read the first question, your mind seems completely empty. You struggle to think of where to begin. Your chest tightens, making it difficult to breathe. You have to fight just to stay in the room and complete the exam.

88

An unrealistic scenario? Not at all. Test anxiety affects the student on physical, emotional, and cognitive levels. It may escalate to a full-blown episode of terror, not unlike the process that occurs in panic disorders. Relatively benign thoughts or physical sensations are interpreted disastrously, leading to an intensifying cycle where anxious fears begin to feed upon themselves. Conquering test anxiety requires many of the same elements used clinically to treat panic disorder.

Since it is impossible to be anxious and relaxed at the same time, the first task in effectively dealing with test anxiety is to interrupt the debilitating physical component. You can do this by practicing a simple technique called the "quieting breath." This exercise should take no more than eight to ten seconds you'll find it works well for all types of anxiety, particularly performance anxiety. One of its advantages is that it is both quickly executed and very effective.

Exercise #1: Close your eyes. Draw in a slow, deep breath to a count of four, then hold it for one to two seconds. Breathe out to a count of four, and again hold your breath for one to two seconds. During the pauses you will notice a brief sense of inner calm. Repeat as often as you feel the need to do so.

The quieting breath may be enough for you to interrupt developing anxiety; or, slightly more extensive techniques may be needed. In 1929, Edmund Jacobson, M.D., wrote a book called Progressive Relaxation. In his book, Jacobson was the first to explore the effect of tension on physical health and to develop a practical method of taking conscious control over muscular tension.

His technique, called "progressive relaxation," shows how to identify where a person holds muscular tension. The individual undertakes a progressive sequence of first tensing then relaxing various muscles. After being held under tension, a muscle lengthens or relaxes to a greater extent than it did prior to the conscious tensing. This teaches the person to identify the feeling within their muscles in a relaxed state. Eventually a person learns how to release tension without having to go through the process of tensing then relaxing each and every muscle.

As is true with any skill, progressive relaxation becomes easier with practice. Full-length scripts of the progressive relaxation technique are available from a variety of sources, including the Internet. Regular daily practice, aside from being fun and relaxing, is required to gain mastery of the skill. The following exercise is a modified progressive relaxation technique for use prior to taking an exam.

Exercise #2: Start by closing your eyes and taking the slow, relaxed breath described in Exercise #1. Are there parts of your body that feel tense, even painful? Where are they? Tilting your head slightly back, shrug your shoulders tightly and hold that shrug for five to ten seconds. Repeat this step once more. Slowly turn your head to the side stretching the muscles in your neck. Repeat this in the opposite direction. Wrap your arms around your upper torso so that your hands touch your shoulder blades. If you can't reach your shoulder blades, comes as close as you can. Slowly twist in one direction and hold for five seconds. Repeat this step in the opposite direction. With your arms still wrapped around your upper torso, drop your chin to your chest and curl your upper body forward. Notice how much looser you feel. This can be complemented by massaging yourself on the neck and shoulders. These steps can be repeated as many times as you feel necessary.

90

For tension in the lower body, bringing your knees up to your chest will stretch out the lower back (wear pants for this one!).

Another technique for conquering test anxiety is cognitive interruption. This occurs well before you meet the challenge of an exam.

Every situation or event in our lives is influenced by our beliefs. Belief can be described as "a strong emotional and cognitive state of certainty." Given the same event, individuals will respond differently based upon their beliefs. When overcome with test anxiety, our beliefs often turn negative, with irrational thoughts cascading through our head. What follows is usually just what we feared. However, when we hold beliefs that are positive in nature, our behavior becomes a reflection of that positive outlook. We are not born with a particular set of beliefs; instead, we develop them through the course of time and experience. Our beliefs exert great power over ourselves and our lives, be it positive or negative. However, what we believe particularly about ourselves and our abilities is not fixed, but changeable.

Exercise #3: The first step to cognitive interruption is to write down all of the negative, irrational self-talk that you have experienced during periods of test anxiety. Take a moment to close your eyes and recall your last test situation. What were your thoughts? What thoughts did you have at the beginning of the process? What did the thoughts develop into? The act of writing down the thoughts, no matter how irrational they might have been, is helpful in that it makes them tangible and more real.

The next step is the cognitive dispute. Take each of the negative and irrational thoughts and write a more reasonable, realistic dispute to them. This is also a step in what is known as "reality testing." If you have studied regularly and effectively, you know that you are well prepared for an exam. This fact allows you to dispute thoughts like "I didn't study hard enough and I'm going to fail." The disputes or reality testing that you develop become the basis for positive statements or affirmations you will use in the next step of conquering test anxiety. Affirmations are best kept brief. "I am well prepared" or "I know I'm going to do well" are good examples of brief affirmations. Write your disputes down following this form of brief but positive affirmation.

Visualization is a performance-enhancing technique used by athletes all over the world. It involves creating mental pictures of a positive outcome. For example, a weight-lifter, just prior to his lift, will imagine seeing himself easily hoist the weight.

As a student, you want to create a mental picture of positive outcomes around your taking a test. You may want to picture yourself calmly completing an exam or perhaps being handed˘back the exam paper with a big red "A" on the top of it. The positive visual picture of a

91

successful outcome is paired with the positive affirmations that you have created in the cognitive disputing step.

As you enter the exam room, as soon as you take your seat, begin the process of overcoming test anxiety. Start with a few repetitions of the quieting breath technique. Continue with the brief progressive relaxation exercise. When you have eliminated the majority of your muscle tension, start visualizing a positive outcome while in your mind repeating your positive affirmations. Throughout this phase, continue using the quieting breath technique. When the test arrives, take a quick, quieting breath and just look the test over. This is a brief skimming of the test format and some of the questions. Determine a question or two to which you readily know the answer, or identify a section that looks particularly easy. You want to start the process with some immediate success. Answer these questions or complete that section of the test then go back to the beginning and start sequentially running through the test. Use the quieting breath as needed to deal with any emerging anxiety.

Anxiety also plays a positive role in any performance situation. It heightens our senses and, if not excessive, can sharpen our recall of information. A certain amount of anxiety is an asset in any performance situation.

And, remember, everyone experiences anxiety. It may not escalate to the full-blown variety of test anxiety we have described here, but it precedes the taking of tests for just about every student.

Although low-level anxiety can be useful, lingering or chronic anxiety prior to a test is downright wearing. An excellent intervention tool is humor. Have on hand a collection of cartoons from a writer you like, but don't read it until you need a humor break so that its impact is fresh. What I call "quick-burst humor," like that found in

92

Dilbert and the The Far Side are particularly effective. Instead of cramming the hour before an exam, use that time to take a humor break. This can be done alone or in a group. Nothing dispels the negative aspects of low-level test anxiety like humor. You will find it not only adds some fun to the testing process but will improve your performance as well.

Notes

Guerrilla Study Techniques

"The test of first-rate intelligence is the ability to hold two opposing ideas in the mind and still retain the ability to function. One should, for example, be able to see that things are hopeless and yet be determined to make them otherwise".

- F. Scott Fitzgerald

The tasks ahead of you seem monumental. How will you complete everything required of you in this academic quarter? The answer is, instead of working harder, you want to work smarter. One way to do that is by employing guerrilla study techniques.

Just what are guerrilla study techniques? The name is taken from a specialized type of combat. Guerrilla soldiers function in small groups. They are rapid, highly mobile attack troops that often take on much larger foes. Guerrilla study techniques allow students to cover a lot of ground very quickly, attacking a large workload with efficient means and then moving on. The following are some strategies that will help you accomplish more is less time.

Churn and Burn Researching

In the beginning of the quarter, you receive a course syllabus advising you of the assigned papers, their topic, and their length. If you have five to ten papers to complete before the end of the quarter, with a requirement of five to fifteen references for each book, that could translate to a lot of library time.

A first question to ask yourself is "Can any of these papers be related?" The answer is often yes. If this is the case, you can target one general subject area or topic and develop variations on the theme for each of the various papers. If you are taking a number of courses in your chosen major, you may even find that you can relate the same topic to different courses. This approach can consolidate both the number of references you need and the reading required. There is no law that says you must use a reference only once.

After you determine how you can interrelate papers in a particular course or courses, take a look at the suggested reading for the course. Are there any summary articles in your reading? Articles that are oriented to overviews of a particular topic are a goldmine for references. They also can suggest areas that you might develop into a paper. Read the overview article and use it to brainstorm related topics for your papers.

Once you have figured out some tentative topics for your papers, turn to the reference section of the overview article. Here you will find a broad number of articles to help you in your research. Make a copy of the reference list, then highlight all of the articles that sound like promising references for your designated papers. Stick this into a folder and mark it "References - Course (which would be the number or title)" and set it aside.

References lists are tremendous resources if you are writing about a little-researched subject. They can also raise a red flag on a topic which may cause you difficulty. For example, a topic that has only one or two references listed may just be too obscure to provide you enough material for a paper. You may want to rethink your choice of subject matter. In the case where there is little written on a particular subject, look at the reference lists for those articles you can find. Those authors had to develop their paper somehow. As suggested, copy the reference lists, mark the ones that show promise, and place them in a folder.

Next, make your initial scouting trip to the library or, if you are on-line with your school's library system, link up through your own computer. Perform your literature search by brainstorming possible key words for your topic. Literature search engines, just like their Internet counterparts, work from key words. Many college libraries have classes on how to use their literature search engine, and I recommend that you take one. They are well worth your time.

Plan on spending a block of time doing nothing but literature searching and gather all your references for all of your papers in one sitting, which is the most efficient use of your time. Everything for one paper or course gets filed at the time it is gathered.

The final fast-strike step requires a partner, either another student, friend, or a family member. You are going to divide and conquer the work of harvesting the reference literature.

I suggest you and your partner attack this task on a low-demand day for the library, usually the weekend. Buy an electronic copy card for the library copy machines or, if your library does not sell copy cards, bring a roll of quarters. Your partner is going to do nothing but copy and file in folders.

Your job will be to search for specific articles. Read the abstract to quickly check as to the appropriateness of the article. Clearly mark the articles you want copied; if you have a reference list, make an additional mark to highlight everything from the same journal, so that you can copy all pertinent articles at one time. If you gather references on a sequential basis, you'll find yourself making trips back and forth to the same place. Like the guerrilla soldier, you want to strike quickly and efficiently.

Working with a partner lets you complete this task in as little as a quarter of the time it would take you if you were to tackle it alone—and you come away with at least 90 percent of what you will need to write your papers. You have everything organized in its own file by course or paper, saving you more time when you go to write the paper. Any additional references can be obtained on an as-needed basis. As you become more proficient with literature searching, you may have little or no need to obtain additional references.

Remember to reciprocate your partner's help. If you were assisted by another student using the same strategy, you can return the favor, making it a mutually rewarding process. If a family member acted as your partner, find a way to show your appreciation. What your partner gave you is extremely valuable to you as a hardworking student—the gift of more time.

Condensed Reading

I often wondered if my professors believed that their course was the only thing I had going in my life. The required reading at the college or graduate level may be equivalent to reading War and Peace several times during the quarter. Some professional programs, such as law and medicine, make very high demands on the student to read and absorb information. Sometimes it is impossible to keep up with the required reading. The reality is that you just can't read every word. So how do you decide what and how you will read?

Start with the core reading for the class. This will be the most information-dense material. Eighty to

90 percent of this material is elaboration on concepts presented in the headings of the chapter. This material merits a more thorough reading than what you will do for the suggested or support literature. Your strategy is to read the first several paragraphs in a section. When the writer moves to material that clearly elaborates on the initial information in that section, move on to the next section.

Support reading is the reading which is not as content-dense and expands on aspects of the core content. These pieces can come from a list of suggested readings given by the instructor or can simply be copied articles rather than the main text. Here is where reading can be condensed.

Research articles begin with an abstract, which gives you a good overall sense of the content of the article. After reading the abstract, move on to the next section of the article, which is the summary or the introduction. This section further defines the problem or issue discussed in the paper. Highlight key phrases in this section.

Continue on to the subsections of the paper. If you think of a paper as presented in an outline format, then each heading introduces a topic or main idea. The main idea of a section is found in the lead sentence of the section. Quickly highlight the main idea of a section and move on the next section. This is known as "fast skimming" and allows you to quickly pull out main ideas. Generally, sections about subject populations and research methods can be paid only cursory attention or skipped entirely. The abstract will often define the subject population and the type of research tool used. If that is the case, make sure the population and method have been highlighted in the abstract —then skip those sections entirely.

The summary or conclusions section merits full reading. This is the essence of what the researcher has found. The organization of this section can be distilled into an outline format. Look for sentences that make a statement. That is where you will find what the researchers believe to be fact, based on their research.

Narrative papers follow the same organization you do when writing a term paper or responding to an essay question. The starting point is an overview of the problem. Highlight the key points and be able to summarize the problem, premise, or issue discussed in the paper. The first subject heading is a clear demarcation of the end of the initial summary of the paper's content. From that point on, the paper can be viewed from an outline perspective with section headings forming the markers for new ideas and content.

100

Each subject heading can be broken down further. The lead sentence states the idea of the paragraph. Here is where the student picks up speed. Underline the idea or concept for a section and then move on. If a section or beginning or a paragraph grabs your interest or seems to have more content in it, by all means, read it all. Keep in mind, however, that your goal is to rapidly move through the meat of the paper to the summary or conclusions section.

In a distraction-free environment, each paper can be reviewed in a range of two to ten minutes. Retention of the material is increased by transferring the information to cards which will be used in other guerrilla techniques. Start by writing the reference at the top of the card. This should follow an approved reference style, such as the one given by a professional association in your field. The reference should be in the format you would use in a bibliography or reference list.

Next, write down what the paper found or concluded, including the name of the population studied. This should be a brief statement. Here is an example:

"Correctional officers have shortened life spans due to occupational stress."

Return to the subsections of the paper to find the factors which support the conclusion. Using the same example, we would list the factors underneath our initial statement that come directly from the subject headings of the paper.

"Correctional officers have shortened life spans due to occupational stress."
- low decision-making autonomy with high-level responsibility. pg. 24
- physically and mentally hostile environment; assault/hostage potential. pg. 26
- little opportunity for advancement. pg. 27
- rigid schedules/shift work; little accommodation for needs of family. pg. 30
- mandatory overtime/working many hours in a week. pg. 31
- isolation from co-workers. pg. 32

101

On the reverse side of the card I will note any sentence that is particularly striking, one that makes some point or conclusion in a clear or compelling manner. This can be used later as a quote in papers or in class discussion.

Writing cards out in this manner will help you in a number of different ways. Your retention of information is going to be minimal if all you do is skim the material. Creating the card allows you to better imprint the material in your memory as well as integrate it with other information. The cards can be quickly reviewed for easy repetition of the information. These cards will also come into play in two other guerrilla techniques.

Class Expert

An academic course can be looked at as an implicit contract between student and instructor, both agreeing to perform their responsibilities to create a successful educational experience. The instructor brings expertise and a prepared presentation to class, creating the opportunity for the student to learn. The student comes to class with assignments completed and prepared to be an active participant in the class. In many classes, discussion makes up a significant part of the time in the classroom and classroom participation can comprise a large part of the overall evaluation of the student. When students come to class hungry for information and ready to actively participate in discussion, the experience is more satisfying for the instructor. Instructors will tend to put more into their presentation when they have a class of students who are active and articulate in their discussion.

Bringing your participation to a higher level builds on the previous guerrilla technique of translating your reading to cards. The "class expert" is really the one who displays the most expertise with the material, and you can achieve this simply by having relevant cards at your fingertips during class discussion, allowing you to reference specific content from your reading. You can also add to your reference cards additional points that come out of the classroom discussion.

Think about the message you send to an instructor when you can reference specific information from suggested or ancillary reading. You make the strong statement that you are a student who is committed to a higher level of understanding and you demonstrate your effort and academic capability in a tangible way. In the competitive world of academics, you distinguish yourself from the other students.

The payoffs from this level of participation are many. First and foremost is your own learning. Actively engaging in thought and discussion of material seats it in memory. The recall is far more potent when you have experienced the level of integration that comes from active discussion. Good grades become a natural conse-quence of putting your learning first.

Opportunity goes to those who are perceived as the most diligent and capable. When you prepare your-self as I have suggested, you demonstrate that you possess both of these attributes. Instructors are often aware of opportunities that may not be open to everyone and can open doors for you that otherwise would be closed if you were viewed as simply one of the herd. Just think how much more powerful a letter of recommendation can be from an instructor whom you have impressed with your preparation and hunger for education. Instructors with whom you have established this kind of relationship may be invaluable assets for future networking when you seek employment.

103

The One-Sitting Paper

The topic of your paper has been decided. Refer-ences have been collected and evaluated. An outline of the main argument of the paper and the factors which support your conclusions has been completed. You are about ready to get started with the actual writing.

Even though you have all of your reference mate-rial at hand, you may find putting your finger on the right piece of information just when you need it to be difficult. More than likely, you have lots of paper with lots of information, all of which you must shuffle through to find the one particular fact you need. The more you look, the more disorganized your pile of papers becomes; soon any semblance of organization is lost as you waste time in your vain search to find that critical fact you know is there somewhere.

Most of us have been down that trail before. Not only is it frustrating, time-consuming, and inefficient, it interrupts the writing process, making it difficult to keep up the flow of the paper.

This is another instance in which you can use guerrilla techniques to work smarter instead of harder.

Take your outline and the cards you made when you were gathering your reference materials. Quickly read through the cards; then, make a note in the margin next to each section of the outline as to which article supports the points in that portion of the paper. Once this is completed, tape up your outline so you can readily refer to it.

Clear off your desk, then place all of the cards on the work space around you. You may wish to organize them based on how you will use the information in the paper. Just as is true of the way the articles are written, 80 to 90 percent of your paper's content will support and embellish upon a particular point or issue in the body of the paper. The substance of that expansion of your outline comes directly from the reference material. With your cards, you have all of the information right at your fingertips.

On your cards, you noted the article and page number where a particular piece of information is referenced. As you move through your paper and want to cite specific material, you select the appropriate folder, go right to the referenced page, and easily access the information. Bodda-boom, bodda-bing! You are back writing right away. You have eliminated the distraction of hunting desperately for pieces of information and are able to maintain your momentum and train of thought.

For every paper you write, you must list the references cited in that paper. This can be a tedious task if you have to go back to the copies of the original material and create the citing for the reference in its correct format. If you made up the reference cards as suggested, however, you already have the information in front of you, presented in the proper format. All you need to do is to arrange the citings in alphabetical order and copy them. Again, you have eliminated the need to search and shuffle through endless piles of papers. When you finish the last reference, you can throw your hands in the air just like a calf roper because you are pretty much done. Don't forget to use the spell check and grammar check. Then, print out a hard copy and put it away for a later reread and perhaps some polishing to tighten up the paper.

Writing a successful paper comes from following a series of well-thought-out steps. Putting the words down on paper develops a flow; what maintains the flow is keeping distractions to a minimum. With the method I have described, you minimize internal distractions and can cut your writing time down to as little as a third of what you used to spend. Again, you are becoming a guerrilla student: lightning fast and ruthlessly efficient in completing your tasks and moving on.

Guerrilla Study Group

Guerrilla study groups have a number of factors in common with guerrilla fighting bands. Both guerrilla soldiers and guerrilla students are bound together by a common goal. Common goals create a powerful degree of motivation supported and reinforced by the group's members. The smallness of the group, be it a group of soldiers or students, is what makes the group highly efficient. There is a minimum of waiting for group members to catch up when moving quickly through enemy territory or study material. Tasks can be divided among members, all aimed at the common good.

Group learning is a synergistic process. We all have our own thoughts about the material to be studied, and the impact of an issue is different for all of us given our varying life experiences. We think in similar, yet unique ways. The advantage of group study is that we can gain perspectives and insights beyond our own.

Several factors surrounding the group process increase motivation. Just like the guerrilla soldiers fighting for a single cause, group studying binds students to a shared goal, a common vision for the outcome of the group's efforts. These mutual goals increase the degree of affiliation and investment of group members, evoking a higher level of expectation about the performance of individual members. This internal dynamic serves to make each individual feel responsible for not letting down the group as a whole. This motivational synergy is extraordinarily powerful, creating an accountability that might not exist when a student studies alone.

Group study moves a student beyond learning through passive reception of information. Like the example from the previous chapter of "see one, do one, teach one," group study involves that final step—teaching. This presses the individual to attain a higher level of understanding of the material. If you want to understand a certain field of study, learn it so well that you can teach it to others. A higher degree of integration and clarity evolves from the challenge of having to explain concepts to others. The division of labor in the guerrilla study group places each individual member in the position of teaching a specific area he or she has researched to others within the group.

I have found that the most effective groups are limited to three or four people; more members can complicate the process and reduce the efficiency of the group. When you study in common areas, classmates you encounter may casually ask to join the group, and you might find it difficult to say no. Because of the focused, task-directed nature of the group, study membership must be fixed. To avoid this kind of problem, find a room free from distractions and the potential for casual membership.

How do you select group members? You want people who will add to the energy and effort of the group. It helps to be a bit of a detective when looking for good studymates. For example, in class, take note as to who is consistently on time. This small factor is often a reflection of a person's work habits and the attitude a student has about their education. Look at where a person sits in class. Unless the instructor has assigned specific seats, where a person chooses to sit is very revealing. There is usually a direct correlation between a person's grades and his proximity to the front of the classroom. The top students sit near the front; they strive to get every bit they can out of the class. More active participation in group discussion is going to come largely from the front half of the class. Less able students are more likely to be found near the back of the room, where they can be passive rather than active participants.

When you ask people if they would like to form a study group, be sure that you discuss the format and expectations of the group members. Sharing the information from this chapter can be a good starting point. The group is going to become an entity: rules and norms for the group will quickly develop. Members must understand and be committed to the process of the group from the beginning if your group study is going to be highly focused and directed. A crucial question for members to answer is whether they can commit to a study group with

107

an active plan for their continued study. The answer must be "yes" for all members, or the group will not accomplish its goal.

Once the group members are established, discussion can turn to how to structure study time. There are many different ways to study. The group may want to use repetition and drill, a useful strategy when faced with having to command a high volume of facts. Or, the class material may lend itself more to group discussion. Courses of study like law often stress integration of material, rather than the recall of facts. Of course, you don't have to stick to just one format; you will probably actually develop a hybrid of several methods of review.

The efficiency of a force of guerrilla soldiers comes from their ability to share responsibilities while developing an expertise in a specialized area. You want members of the study group to function like this as well. You accomplish this by assigning duties to each member of the group. Divide up the material to be covered for each week and determine who will run each meeting, making sure this is done on a rotating basis. As the leader, each member will have the opportunity to step into the role of teacher, sharing the information he or she has acquired during the week.

In the week prior to your turn as the study group leader, you will have more preparation for the meeting than usual. The good news is that you only have to do this a quarter of the time. You can prepare by writing down potential study questions as you go through your reading. Do this by asking yourself "If I were the teacher, what would I ask my students to test their knowledge?" As you come up with relevant questions, you spontaneously start to think about how you would answer them. Moving into this role of teacher forces you to attain a higher level of integration—you must push yourself to take that important step beyond just absorbing the

108

information. You will find that the material you present when it is your turn to run the study group will become the material you understand most solidly.

A few days prior to the exam, the group should run a review session that encompasses all of the information. Resist the temptation to do this the day before the test. Each person runs the part of the total review for which he or she was responsible. This session requires no additional work, but is simply a review of what you have already covered. After this review is completed, the members move to individual study using whatever means works best for them.

If schedules can be coordinated to squeeze in a short review on the day of the exam, it will take a different format. Each member is encouraged to bring up one or two areas for final clarification, keeping discussion brief and specific. This is not a time for repetition and drill, as the pressure created by this type of last-minute review is more likely to increase pretest stress.

109

I find a good way to cap off the final pretest meeting is to use humor to diffuse tension. During one of my pretest review sessions in graduate school, a group of us sat around sharing books by various cartoonists, which gave us all a much-needed laugh. Laughter has an amazing power to relax both mind and body. You know the material at this point; and if you don't, it's too late. Some of the material you probably know so well you could even teach it. Time to let go, clear out the brain, and get loosened up for the test.

The need to debrief after a difficult challenge is a natural way to relieve the stress of the experience. Coming out of the class, the first thing people ask each other is how they did on the test and what the answer to a particular question was. Your study group may or may not want to debrief as a group after the exam. Decide this before you take the exam. If you decide to get together, make it a time to let down, to offer support and encouragement to other group members. The last thing you want to do is to extend your anxiety about the test.

If you decide to let down after a test on your own, know what will help you decompress most effectively. You might find exercise a good relaxant; maybe you just need to "veg out" in front of the TV. Decompressing is an important component of the study dynamic, as you have to wind down before you can move on to the next challenge. Take some time to discover what works best for you.

Power Presentations

The number-one fear most people admit to having is the fear of public speaking. Coming in second is fear of death. Comedian Jerry Seinfeld points out that if you're at a funeral, this means you'd rather be the person in the box than the one giving the eulogy.

Giving presentations is an unavoidable requirement of most educational programs. For many people, the prospect of standing up in front of peers and professors alike provokes extreme anxiety. The fight-flight response erupts in full force: your mouth goes dry, your voice quavers, your heart races, you feel like you have to go to the bathroom, you wonder how you will ever get through your presentation. Rest assured, even the best speakers have experienced high anxiety when giving a speech.

A starting point for giving effective presentations is gaining control of your apprehension. In talking about test anxiety in the previous chapter, I gave several exercises for controlling anxiety. The quieting breath is a highly useful exercise for dealing quickly with an anxious state. Inserting a notation in your presentation notes to pause and take a breath is a useful way to not only control anxiety but pace a presentation.

I remember my first professional for-pay presentation. I was to give a forty-five minute talk to a group of parents from the Head Start Program. I had prepared what I considered to be about a forty-minute talk, leaving five minutes for questions and answers. My anxiety level was so high that I raced through my presentation, finishing in about fifteen minutes. I had a moment of utter horror when I realized that I had another thirty minutes to fill. Thinking quickly, I divided the parents into small groups for discussion of a hastily devised question, which ate up some time. I vowed never to repeat that experience again. This didn't mean I was giving up on public speaking. In fact I've gone on to conduct workshops with audiences of over 250 people. It did mean, however, that I needed to learn some things about presentations.

111

The most effective presentations use all of the receptors. You want people to look, listen, and feel. The most successful speakers understand that the average attention span for an audience of a presentation is only about ten to fifteen minutes. The dryer the material, the shorter the attention span. If the speaker is especially engaging or the subject is of particular interest, a listener may be able to focus for as long as twenty minutes before losing concentration.

One way to increase attention span is by switching between receptor pathways. The most effective presentations get people up and moving at regular intervals. Elementary education teachers are perhaps most aware of this need to move, as nowhere are the limits on attention more noticeable than with children. The effective teacher finds ways to let students stand, stretch, and move around. Even though our attention span increases as we get older, we still need to move around or we lose our focus.

Some of the most effective and charismatic speakers can be found on televised religious programs. They are masters of playing to all receptor pathways. They vary the cadence of their voice; they use lavish backdrops; they interrupt their talks with a song from the choir that is vibrantly alive in both auditory and visual components.

Spend some time watching a few of these programs. They can teach you much about the dynamics of public speaking. Many motivational speakers use the very same techniques. People leave not only with useful information, they also feel charged up, excited, alive. Although you may not need to have your audience feel energized in this way, you do want to hold their attention.

Verbal Presentation

112

The most difficult task for the new speaker is how to evenly pace a presentation. The mistake I made in rushing through my presentation is very common. New speakers have a tendency to speed up when they talk because they're in such a hurry to get it over with. Here are a few pointers to keep you from falling into that trap.

Preparing your notes properly can help you slow down your presentation. Notes should not be used to tell you exactly what to say; they act as reminders of what to talk about regarding your content. Although you do not want to read your presentation, there are two exceptions to this rule: the beginning sentence for your main points and exact quotes.

Start your notes by writing down the salutation or first sentence of your presentation in bold, block letters at least half an inch high. You want to be able to see your notes just by glancing down at them. At the end of this first spoken line, write "PAUSE!" The purpose of the pause is twofold. It gives you time to compose yourself and relax, providing the perfect interval for taking a quieting breath. You also give your audience time to absorb what you have said.

The next part of your presentation notes contains different pieces of information to underscore or support the main point. These are brief, as you should be familiar enough with your subject that a short reminder is all you need to launch you into talking about your subject.

Just as in written work, 80 to 90 percent of a speech is embellishment of the main points of the presentation. In a thirty-minute presentation, you may make as few as three main points. More technical presentations may make five to seven main points. Be aware that too much core content can overwhelm an audience. Your presentation will be seen as more effective if you present fewer main ideas and then effectively expand on those ideas.

113

We spend a good portion of our day talking with others. When we give a presentation, our anxiety erases the idea that the essence of what we are doing is just talking with people. If we view our speech as directed conversation, we can certainly eliminate some of our apprehension. There are a number of techniques speakers can use to overcome audience intimidation; for example, some speakers picture their audiences as wearing funny glasses and noses or wearing only their underwear. You can learn more by doing some research on the art of successful presenting.

Another helpful technique is making eye contact with members of the audience. At first you might think this would be distracting to you as the speaker. Instead, it actually keeps you moving along at a easy, steady pace. Think of it as similar to what you do when you're driving. You often check the rearview and side mirrors or glance to your left or right. Your attention is not diverted; instead, you have a better overall idea of what kind of conditions you're driving in because of these brief scannings.

As you learn to incorporate making eye contact into your presentations, you may want to try putting a colored dot at regular intervals on your presentation notes. This can provide a visual cue to pause, take a breath, or make eye contact. I generally make five to ten eye contacts per minute during a presentation, which means that I don't spend very long looking at one person. In larger groups, the duration of the eye scan lengthens, as you want to make sure eye contact is established. Using this technique, you can give the members of larger audiences the feeling that your presentation is quite personal. Nothing makes a speech seem more wooden that a speaker who doesn't make eye contact with the audience.

114

Practice your presentation by watching and listening to yourself in front of a mirror. Saying the words out loud lets your ear tell you whether your initial sentence is clear and understandable. If the sentence is awkward and doesn't readily flow, you want to fix it now. Once you're up in front of your audience, it will be too late.

How do you look when you are giving your presentation? Are you fixed and rigid? Do you nervously fidget with your hands? Ninety percent of communication is nonverbal, so what your body expresses is extremely important. Spend some time observing people in ordinary conversation. You will notice that they are constantly moving. Many people not only move their head, but also their hands, arms, shoulders, even bodies when they're talking.

What movements do you make when you're speaking? As you repeatedly practice your presentation, start incorporating eye scan and hand movements. Find what feels natural, for that is the key. You will make giving—and listening to—your presentation easier for both you and your audience.

Have you ever wondered how comedians can recall an hour of material and give it just the right timing so the presentation is funny? The answer is practice—lots and lots of practice. You need to do the same if you want your presentation to be fresh, interesting, and worth listening to.

Visual Presentation

We have discussed adding dimension and life to your verbal presentation. Visual presentation can add interest and increase your audience's attention span as well.

Some speakers use handouts to create visual interest. I feel these distract the audience. When people transfer their attention to the handout, they take it away from you. Slides, computer-generated programs with graphics, even videos can be useful in adding a positive visual dimension to a presentation. In an academic setting, these types of visuals should be brief and only used as a support to your speech. You want the presentation to reflect your work, not the work of the artist or videographer.

Physical Pathways

Ever notice what happens during a long class when the instructor goes past the usual break time? People start shifting in their chairs; they look up at the clock; they start to whisper among themselves. In short, they lose their ability to pay attention.

Whenever possible, you want to get people moving at some point during the course of the presentation.

115

If you can't reasonably get people to stand up and move, have them handle things. Years ago, I was in a lecture on sensory changes with advanced age. The presenter handed out cheap sunglasses smeared with Vaseline which we put on. He had us tape pieces of cotton on our fingertips and then put rubber gloves on our hands. We stuffed our ears with cotton balls. The presenter then asked us to do simple activities like picking up coins, reading normal-sized print, and having a conversation.

This exercise communicated more about the sensory changes in the elderly than any amount of talking would have accomplished. We learned on an experiential level. That learning was powerful and long-lasting; it also broke up the presentation by interjecting something other than verbal information. The element of fun lightened what could have been a very dry subject.

116

Inserting a physical element into a presentation is a challenge to your creativity, but it can be an immensely powerful addition. A presentation that makes a few points effectively will be better received than one that covers more information but loses the audience in the process.

Handouts

As mentioned before, handouts can add a useful dimension to a presentation, but they often distract attention from the speaker. One effective way to use handouts is to pass them out early in the presentation, letting your audience know that the information you'll be giving is outlined for them. Leave plenty of space for your audience to write notes on the outline. There are people who, no matter how thoroughly you have outlined your topic, have a compulsion to write things down. Your goals are to minimize the amount of writing the audience has to do.

Handouts can also be helpful in giving your audience a resource list. This may include specific literature or phone numbers and addresses where people can call or write to get free information. And don't forget the Internet. In this age of information, there are websites for just about everything. A quick search on the Internet will give depth to your resource list. Your audience will appreciate any information you can give them to lessen the time they have to spend tracking it down themselves.

117

Notes

118

Motivation

Your pathway to higher education is illuminated by the bright vision you have for yourself and your future. If, when you enter the academic vortex, you bring with you an established life filled with the commitments of family and a career, you place yourself in a situation where your inner resources will be rigorously tested. Whether your course through school lasts one year or ten, you still need to sustain yourself economically, physically, emotionally, and spiritually to withstand the demands that will continually be made upon you.

You may ask yourself, "How am I going to do all of this?" In using this book, you will learn a number of skills and techniques to help you succeed in managing the profusion of demands that school will place upon you.

The larger question to ask is "How will I sustain myself through the long haul of completing school?" There will be times when you question whether the academic process you have begun is right for you, whether you can continue juggling all of the balls that you have in the air.

These challenges will define what motivates you. What fuels and sustains you as an individual? What do you need and value in your life? When you figure out the answer to those questions, when you know with certainty what is important to you, then you will be motivated.

School can offer a certain gratification that you can't get at home or at work; that can be intoxicating. It can also be just a means to an end in your journey to fulfill the vision that you carry for yourself. Whatever role it plays, it's helpful to remember that school is just one chapter in your life, not the whole book.

A fundamental belief I held when I was struggling with sustaining a family, holding down a job, and pursuing an education was that if I lost what was important to me as a result of school, I would not be a success, even if I finished at the top of my class.

120

Determine what is most important to you, and then allow your natural excitement and interest to motivate you to pursue that dream.

Values

He who knows much about others may be learned, but he who understands himself is more intelligent. He who controls others may be powerful, but he who has mastered himself is mightier still.
            -Lao-Tsu, Tao Teb King

Everyone entering school has their own unique reasons for being there. In my practice, I often tell my younger clients about the usefulness of having a job that they hate. The prospect of a future asking people if they would like fries with their burger can be a powerful motivator. We often find the will to change through our reaction to negative influence.

Your vision for your future may be a reflection of the person you hope to be. The same adjectives you might use to describe the profession you seek may be the very same ones that describe the person you want to become. The direction we choose in our careers is an outgrowth of our beliefs about ourselves and the person we see ourselves to be both now and in the future.

We are guided by our values, whether they are known to us consciously or lie buried in our subconscious. Values that are not readily identified exert just as power-ful a force in guiding our decisions as those we are aware of. Our values are a powerful motivational tool. If we first understand what our values are and clarify their meaning in our lives, then we can support those values in the course of our education. Success is ultimately depen-dent upon keeping and supporting the values we hold as most basic in our lives.

Values are loaded with emotion. They evoke a strong visceral response, be it positive or negative. To motivate someone, you must first understand what that person values. When you understand the values of another person, you can evoke a positive emotional response. This response is the essence of motivation. It works not only with others, but also with yourself.

Few things we experience in life contain the power of those emotions generated by acting in accordance with our values. This is what makes us feel good about what we do in our lives, the very foundation of self-satisfaction. We inherently seek activities which are reinforced by the generation of positive emotions.

The opposite is just as true. If what we do has no congruence with our values, we have little chance of being motivated to continue those activities. Have you ever been in a job that on a fundamental level went against your basic values? I had a client who felt his values supported the selection of work as a stockbroker. He wanted to provide more financial support for his family. Making more money meant that his family could have many of the things he didn't have when he was growing up. The financial rewards of work as a stockbroker held the promise of what he saw as a better life. Seeking this kind of life for both his family and himself created a powerful, emotion-laden force to change careers. This value became a powerful tool for change.

For my client to become a licensed stockbroker required a high level of study. Much of the material was quite dry and very detailed. But the vision he held for his future sustained him through the tedious process of preparing for the licensing exam, which he passed on the first try. He subsequently found work in a successful brokerage house and felt he had succeeded in fulfilling his dream.

122

After six months working as a stockbroker, he became painfully aware of how much he hated it. He had begun to work sixty to seventy hours a week, a practice that would be expected of him for the rest of his working life. This would mean that his children would grow up with a father who was largely absent from active involvement in their lives. Because his own father had been similarly absent during his own childhood, my client held involvement in his children's lives as a strong value.

Another of his values was being violated in his work as a broker. He often was instructed to buy or sell a particular stock, even though he felt it might not be the best choice for the investor. He found himself in a position where he had to ignore his value of doing what he felt to be in the best interests of a client, simply because it was his job to do what he was told. This compromised a strong ethical value he held.

This was an emotionally intense time because this man had two sets of values pulling him in two different directions: the desire for more income and a more comfortable life for his family versus the desire to spend more time with his family and perform a service for his clients. The stronger values won out. The incongruence he experienced with the values of family involvement and serving his clients' best interests motivated him to abandon a career for which he had worked so hard.

This story illustrates how values you hold can have a hierarchy of importance. My client misinterpreted which values were strongest within his life, leading to his choice of an incongruent career. Knowing what you value and then pursuing a lifestyle that supports those values can provide you the motivation to work through school. Remembering all of the values you hold will help you maintain balance in life. Making sure you allot time for all the important aspects of your life allows you to enjoy the process of school more. If the important core values in your life are ignored, you will eventually resent the demands of school. School becomes much like a sentence to be served rather than a process which expands the growing edges of your life. You will find yourself losing the motivation to continue the process.

How do we discover what our hierarchy of values is? First you must realize that you have several hier archies of values operating simultaneously. Each has their own context. The values you have in your relation-ships are somewhat different from the ones you hold in your career, although there can be some overlapping or mirroring of the two sets of values. For example, the value of fidelity, which is important in a relationship, can be translated as being true to your word in a business context.

123

Let's start the process of discovering your values hierarchies by looking first at your relationship with the important people in your life. Begin with your partner. Close your eyes and form a mental picture of your partner. Think of some of the times during which you felt particularly good about the relationship. Take time to recollect good times that you haven't thought about for a long time. When you are ready, take a large piece of paper and list the values that have emerged from this process. The list may include things like love, respect, honesty, common spiritual beliefs, support. Don't limit yourself in what you write. This is a brainstorming session; effective brainstorming includes putting down even those things that initially seem silly or trivial.

Now rank the values in order of importance. Start with the first two values on the list. For example, is love more important than respect? Then put them in that order. Continue to compare all of the values to one another. You will eventually form an ordered list of the values you hold to be important in your relationships. This process will no doubt evoke a lot of thought about the relationships in your life, and strong emotions will emerge. Allow yourself to feel these emotions as part of the exercise; they will help you in your determination of your hierarchies.

The next step is to figure out how these values are experienced on a behavioral level. How do you know that you are loved? What does your partner do that allows you to feel loved on an experiential basis? What do you do that communicates to your partner or children that they are loved? If you are in a process of change, you have to be able to recognize when you have gotten what you want. Values can be as ephemeral as the mist until you think about how they are actualized. Writing the behaviors beside the value makes them more tangible, easier to grasp in a functional way.

Now let's repeat the process in another context: school. Your choice to enter school is motivated by a vision that you have for your future, probably an outgrowth of your work experience, both positive and negative. Like the carrot and the stick, we choose change because we want to move away from what we don't like and toward the bright hopes that we have for our future.

Take some time to form an image of the best day that you ever had at work. What was it about that day that made the experience so good? How did you feel? How did you perceive yourself as being? You want to form a mental picture of specific positive experiences. The day that you imagine may actually be a combination of several days or even a particular time in your life.

Take another sheet of paper and list the values that you feel were supported in your image of the best day at work. These values may be similar to the ones you formed when thinking about your relationships. Others will be quite different. This demonstrates how our values exist within a context. For example, take the value of "challenge": In the workplace it has an entirely different meaning and emotional load than the concept of "challenge" in a relationship with our children.

125

Again, you are going to rank the list that you create in order of importance. Just like the previous list of values in relationships, you want to think about the behaviors that supported the values you consider important. Write these behaviors beside the corresponding value.

The next step in the process is to look at both lists side by side. To help you evaluate these lists, I'd like you to think a moment about the viewpoint of existentialist philosophy. One of the tenets of existentialism is that life has meaning because it is finite. We strive to fulfill the purpose of our lives because we are granted only so much time to live. Our children provide compelling examples of this. They seem to grow up so very quickly; each day with them is an opportunity not to be missed.

As you review the lists, think of what values you need to experience to feel you have lived one day to its fullest. Now think of the values that you would support if you knew your life were to end in five years.

The values on the list for living one day to its fullest would probably be skewed toward relationships. The somewhat longer perspective of five years would contain more elements of your work or professional life. In regarding these two finite periods of time, these two different perspectives, you can develop a good sense of the values that are important for you and will help you sustain yourself through the course of your education.

126

One of the most stressful events for a relationship comes with the decision of one partner to go to school. This creates the unavoidable consequence of making that partner less available. The student's time is not just physically unavailable due to class and study time, but to a degree psychologically less available as well. School can devour a person's physical, emotional, and mental energy.

I suggest that you ask your partner to read this chapter and to take the time to clarify his or her values, to explore the specific behaviors that allow him or her to experience those values, just as you have done. Then you and your partner can set aside some quiet time to work together on clarifying your values. You may share many of the same values; you may also find surprising differences. For example, the behaviors that communicate to each of you that you are loved may be quite different. Sharing your values, and the behavior that supports them, opens the door to direct communication about what each of you needs to sustain the relationship through a time that will place great stress upon it.

With this exercise, you and your partner can anticipate how the process of school will bring change into the day-to-day functioning of your relationship. Identifying the concerns before they arise allows you to problem-solve before a crisis emerges, to develop ways that you can continue to nurture one another (and your children if you have them) during this demanding time in your life. Simple things like eating dinner together as a family or designating time to spend focused on your children will help support all of you. You may want to identify particular times during the week where school gets placed on the back burner and meeting the needs of your partner and family becomes your focus.

A trade-off of this planning is that spontaneity can suffer. This is particularly true regarding intimacy in a relationship. If children are part of the equation of your life, that makes it all the more important to plan time for you and your partner to be alone. But keep in mind that you don't want to fall into an unimaginative routine. Draw on your creativity to keep your time together fresh, exciting, even unpredictable, to explore the each other's dreams and desires. You both need that kind of nurturing if you want your relationship to continue to expand and be fulfilling.

Beliefs

> *We are who we think ourselves to be.*
> *-Anonymous*

We think of beliefs as major principles that influence our lives. Faith is an example of one of these guiding principles. Beliefs act as a filter through which we experience the world, including how we see ourselves in the world. They are the guiding force in our behavior.

Beliefs often are neither rational nor logical. Faith, as a guiding belief, has no rational basis: it fails the test of logic. Although it is neither logical nor rational, faith has, in its many varied forms, influenced the lives of millions through the course of time.

Belief operates within us all. Belief is the lantern which guides our vision to future goals, generating the conviction that energizes us to reach them. Its power is enormous. Christopher Columbus was guided by his convictions, although they flew in the face of the universal beliefs both science and government espoused at the time: that the world was flat. Imagine the power of his belief, so strong that he would risk falling off the edge of the earth to challenge the laws of reality of his time. Our own internal beliefs have no less power.

Our beliefs often form very early in our lives and can become more self-limiting as time goes on. If you were to ask a class of first graders how many of them would like to join you in a fifty-mile hike, every hand in the room would go up. If you asked the same question of a group of sixth graders, some hands would go up, some hands would stay down. Ask this same question of a groups of adults and the likelihood is that few, if any, hands would be raised, because many would not believe they could accomplish that goal.

Our lives often teach us to believe in what we can't do rather than empowering us to believe in what we can do. For first graders, personal power is unlimited. They can do whatever they choose to do because they believe that they can. Pablo Picasso named the problem quite simply. He wrote, "Every child is an artist. The problem is how to remain an artist once he grows up." As children we consider life to be our canvas, and we take delight in filling it in as we wish. We might use the color purple to draw a cow or stick a fish in the branch of a tree. Life teaches us that we must color only within the lines, that cows come in brown, black, or white—never

128

purple—and that birds, not fish, belong in trees. In other words, we learn limits.

Our beliefs grow from many sources. The direct and subtle messages we receive from parents, teachers, and other influential people we encounter as we develop often determine how we view ourselves as adults, affecting our basic sense of competency and self-esteem. As a child, when we absorb others' perceptions of us, we start to form a picture of ourselves based on those attitudes. When the messages we receive as we develop are negative, they become limiting factors which rob us of our personal power and lead to our holding irrational beliefs about ourselves.

How we have developed our belief system affects our behavior, which means different people will react differently to the same stimulus, such as stress. Let's take the example of giving critical feedback about a paper to two different students. The first person has a belief system which supports the concept that making mistakes is an acceptable component of the learning process. The second person has a belief system which says that making a mistake is evidence of failure. You can easily see how different belief systems lead to different behavioral and emotional outcomes. Belief becomes a state of being. It is that internal representational system which governs behavior.

Negative beliefs are the ultimate in self-fulfilling prophesies. Consider the person who feels he is not as capable a student as his peers. There is the expectation that no matter how hard he tries, he is not going to do as well as everyone else. Will that person find himself energized by the tasks ahead of him? Of course not! He has created an expectation of failure before he has even started. Is it a realistic measure of what this person is capable? Probably not.

The saving grace of beliefs is that they are not fixed. How you see yourself is not carved in stone. While beliefs may feel like they are fixed and unchangeable, it is only the emotion that is connected with them that makes them feel that way.

One way to challenge your belief system is through Rational Emotive Therapy (RET). Albert Ellis, founder of RET, believed that although people have the capacity for rational thinking, they can fall victim to irrational beliefs which stem from their childhood. These beliefs are sustained by both the uncritical acceptance of these beliefs and by self-talk which continues to confirm these beliefs. The foundation of his theory is that we can evaluate, analyze, and restructure these beliefs. This becomes the basis of behavioral change.

130

Take some time to think about your inner self— your critical self which judges you harshly. You may find that the opinions held deep within you are a reflection of those held by important people in your past. If your perception of yourself is negative, you rob yourself of personal power. What are five beliefs that grow from this negative part of your inner thoughts? Write them down.

1. _____
2. _____
3. _____
4. _____
5. _____

Notice what emotions are evoked when you write down these innermost thoughts. Now focus on just one of these beliefs. Close your eyes and reflect on how that belief makes you feel. The emotion you experience at this moment is not as strong as when you experience it in a real-life situation. Negative emotions are often the logical consequence of irrational beliefs you hold about yourself.

They are as much an outcome as the behaviors which are driven by the emotions.

Many of us have been taught that we shouldn't have negative emotions. Let's face it: negative emotions are an unavoidable fact of life. It's how we deal with negative emotions that is important. The best and fastest way to banish these demons is to express them. When we express these emotions, we take a step toward acceptance which diminishes their power over us.

Write down those emotions evoked by your list of negative, irrational thoughts.

1._____
2._____
3._____
4._____   131
5._____

When we express our emotions, it discharges emotional energy. Consider the universal human experience of trying to hold back tears so as not to embarrass ourselves—when what we most need to do is shed them. This denial of crying takes enormous energy. Think back to a time when you found yourself in this situation. Recall what it felt like when you allowed yourself that release. Recall the sense of relief when you stopped. Because emotions cause a visceral response, it takes immense amounts of energy to contain those emotions.

Let's try an exercise to overcome your negative beliefs. You want to engage the rational, reasonable part of yourself. You may find it useful to imagine yourself as older and wiser, perhaps a "future you" who has learned many more of life's lessons and can act as a wise mentor to yourself. Take a look at each of your irrational beliefs. What would be a more rational reasonable view of these beliefs?

Irrational beliefs tend to have an all-inclusive, absolute quality about them: "I always...," "I can never...." Their very one-sidedness is part of what makes them irrational. People are never one particular way all of the time. You have had countless experiences which dispute these beliefs. It is these experiences of being different that will allow you to effectively challenge your negative beliefs.

Write down the challenges and disputes to your negative beliefs.

1._____
2._____
3._____
4._____
5._____

132

Out of the challenge of irrational beliefs grows the suggestion of different, more positive beliefs. Think about how life would be different if you operated with a more positive belief system.

You have recently made a very empowering decision. You decided to change the course of your life. Like Columbus sailing toward the edge of the world, you decided to risk an unknown and uncertain future. You chose the challenge of school based upon a number of positive beliefs. One of those positive beliefs is that you can control the direction of your future. You have demonstrated that you recognize beliefs to be a choice that you make.

Affirmations

Affirmations are like prescriptions for certain aspects of yourself you want to change.
-Jerry Frankhauser

The difficulty in turning around negative thoughts lies in the fact that over time we become very good at promoting negativity. Our internal critic arises from our unconscious need to discount the positives that we receive. Have you ever had difficulty accepting a compliment? Our internal self has ways of devaluing compliments. We tell ourselves, "Oh, he was just saying that" or "She probably says that to everyone." Think back to a compliment that you discounted. Was the person insincere in their comment? Was he or she indeed "just saying that?" Of course not. He gave you positive feedback because he meant it.

A technique often used in group psychotherapy with depressed people is "the compliment circle." It illustrates and helps people to reality-test the negative critic that lies within. Group members take turns writing down something positive they have experienced with another group member and then read it to the group member to whom it is directed. The receiver of the compliment can give one of three responses:

1. Thank you.
2. I liked hearing that.
3. Say that again.

Members explore whether they thought the compliment was insincere and then ask the member who gave the compliment if she indeed meant what she said. Group members become aware of how uncomfortable it can feel to give a positive accepting response to a compliment.

Try giving one of these three responses the next time you receive a compliment. Notice what you feel. If you feel a bit uncomfortable, then your internal critic is alive and well and working to diminish positive feelings about yourself.

133

Affirmations are positive statements that we make to ourselves, about ourselves. They reflect beliefs. It's true that we may not feel as though we have accepted that belief when we start out saying the affirmation, but it gives us a focus from which that change of behavior can emerge. As we experience a change in our behavior, the belief becomes internalized.

When my son was a toddler, I experienced a lot of frustration in my parenting. I struggled with the lack of patience I had dealing with normal two-year-old behavior. The use of affirmations gave me a focus that also led me to both reflection on and correction of the behaviors with which I was dissatisfied. Affirming to myself that "I can be more patient" allowed me to step back from the situation and stop acting so impatiently and abrupt with my son. I would carry this thought for the day with me, reflecting upon it as needed. It quelled the internal critic that both negated what I was doing well and pointed out where I was failing as a parent.

134

Let me just warn you right now: When you first start working with affirmations, they are going to sound dumb. You might find them silly and embarrassing or they may strike you as stilted and artificial. What's interesting is that we don't feel the same way when we beat ourselves up with negative affirmations: "I'm not smart enough/not young enough/not old enough/not pretty enough/not as good as everyone else..." ad infinitum all come easily to us. But saying something positive is tremendously hard to do.

To summarize, our behavior is an outcome of our beliefs. To change our behavior, we need to first work on our beliefs. Many of our beliefs are irrational and stem from a variety of negative messages from our past. They are internalized in an all-inclusive manner. However, beliefs are not fixed and unchangeable. We must work to test our beliefs, then find new ones that will empower us.

These new, positive beliefs become part of how we think, which in turn allows us to change our behaviors and, ultimately, our experiences for the better.

Self-Reinforcement

> *Whenever personal worth is dependent upon performance, personal value is subject to cancellation with every misstep.*
> *- Dorothy Corkille Briggs*

A great deal of how we form as people is the result of reinforcement. Reinforcement can be both positive and negative. Dorothy Corkille Briggs, a truly exceptional writer and parent educator, writes, "Every child seeks a self picture as capable and strong. And behavior matches self-image." As adults we seek the same image of ourselves. One source of how we view ourselves is found in the external reinforcement that we receive for our behaviors. This confirmation comes from a variety of sources and is important for both children and adults. Have you ever worked for a boss that never said anything good about your work? Without positive feedback from your boss, the workplace feels like a negative hostile place. Any feedback is likely to be experienced as critical. Conversely, a consistent feature of corporations viewed as the best companies to work for is that managers tell employees what they are doing right.

135

We live in an imperfect world. Our parents, partners, children, and supervisors may not realize the effort that went into doing a really good job on a paper, or a project, or a report. If we depend solely on external reinforcement to help support and confirm our positive self-image, we are going to be disappointed. That's why it is so important that we develop internal reinforcement.

Internal reinforcement is that which comes from within ourselves. It is the self-satisfaction that allows us to do a little end-zone dance in our heads when we receive a test back and have done well. The difficulty in keeping up this internal positive reinforcement comes when our sense of worth is contingent on the absolute of how we perform. School is as much a process as it is the acquisition of knowledge and skills. It is the mastery of the process which forms us and allows us to grasp strategies to attack problems both in our professional and personal lives. Corporations realize this. Often when they stipulate that they want a job applicant to have a bachelor's degree, they don't much care what field the degree is in. They recognize that a person is changed by the process. Part of the process of learning is making mistakes and then learning from those mistakes. It makes sense to reward not only the results, but the ability to master the process as well.

136

Like the bad employer, we often have difficulty giving ourselves positives for our work. It may not be enough to just say to ourselves that we did a good job. Tangible rewards are enormously powerful in self-reinforcement. They provide a way of nurturing ourselves, like a bonus that affirms from an internal point of view that our work is worthwhile and valued.

Rewarding your efforts doesn't mean spending a lot of money on yourself. Rewards can be time spent doing fun things that you might otherwise pass up to focus on studies. They can be small gifts, like a special pen or a book that you read for pure enjoyment. What they symbolize is far more important than their monetary value. They represent in a concrete way your affirmation to yourself that you have done a good job.

Self-rewarding needs to be a liberal and frequent endeavor. It should come after you have put in a hard day of work churning out a term paper, or after you have put in a solid week where you felt you sustained your best efforts. How many times have you (or will you) sit for hours on end working on a school project? Your eyes become blurry and tired. Your back and shoulders ache and stiffen up. Your mind lapses into fatigue. Reward yourself with some time watching a game on TV or taking a walk with your partner. These kinds of rewards also help you wind down after sustaining a high level of intensity. The key is to remember that you are doing this to reward yourself for a job well done.

Goals

People are not lazy. They simply have impotent goals—that is, goals that don't inspire them.
- Anthony Robbins

Dig out your dreamer's hat. Sharpen your pencil or turn on the computer. You are going to receive a magic wand that requires you only to think, to dream, and to write down those dreams. This is your chance to give substance to that vision of the future which has illuminated your path toward more education. Now is the time you think about what you want—not only for yourself, but for your family too. It is time not just to dream, but to bring those dreams into focused clarity in the form of tangible goals.

To take full advantage of this process, you want to be very relaxed. Plan for a time when you are well-rested. Get yourself comfortable in the spot where you do your writing. Have a cup of coffee or tea by your side. Make sure you have eaten. Put on some relaxing music. Pick a time where you will be free of distractions. Put aside the "yes, but..." internal critic that is obsessively practical and constraining. Put aside the "voice of past experience" that dashes hopes for a new future. This is a time to get in touch with the child within you who readily raises her hand to go on a fifty-mile hike.

137

You are about to pick up the magic wand that can change your future. That magic wand has a name— it is "I am in control of my own future." You have taken the first step in waving that magic wand by going to school. You have pointed yourself on a course to obtain new knowledge, skills, and experiences. Already some part of you has felt empowered to wave the wand and take this step. This is the part of you that you need to call forward now.

This is a time to put limitations aside. Believe that there is no ceiling on what you can achieve. This does not mean, however, that you can be completely unreasonable. If you can't ice skate, the odds are good that you will never play in the National Hockey League. To hope for something that is completely unattainable drains your creative energy and distracts you from your real dreams and goals. Focus on stretching previous limits and boundaries you have put on your life and your career. The only way you can expect to get what you want is to decide what it is that you want.

This technique is somewhat like a strategy for thinking called "the nursing process." The first step of the nursing process is to define the problem. For you this step would be to define your goal. What do you want to happen in your life? Where do you want to be in your career? You want your answers to these questions to be positive statements. All too often we state our goals in terms of what we don't want; we may not even realize that what we're saying is not positive, we have become so used to phrasing our goals that way. "I don't want to continue to work nights" sounds like a positive statement, yet all it says is what is not wanted. "I want to work nine to five, Monday through Friday" might be the positive corollary to that negative statement.

Now you are going to color in the specifics of the outcome that you desire. Borrowing from clinical

138

hypnosis, describe to yourself not only what the goal is but what it feels like and how it looks. You want to tap all of the sensory outlets for your goals that you can. Paint the goal as a vivid auditory, visual, and kinesthetic experience, which will make the desire more real for your brain and provide unconscious motivation toward meeting that goal. You want the goal to live in your mind, and an enriched sensory description will contribute to this.

Goals need to be focused and specific. One way to do this is to give a goal a timeline. Your goals may have a range of timelines, from a week to a year to ten years. Decide on a completion date for each of your goals and put them in writing.

You have defined your goals and given them a timeline. The next step in the nursing process is to take each goal and devise an agenda and a step-by-step plan for that agenda that will lead you to realizing your goal. Start by asking the question "How am I going to get what I want?" Every goal requires actions you need to take to reach the goal. Some of them may seem painfully obvious, and some goals require more steps and more time. But each step you take is important in achieving your goal, all the more so when the goal is large and in the distant future. When you can break down what might seem like an intimidating goal into smaller steps, you realize that you can reach it. You tell yourself that you can do it—an opportunity for positive self-talk—and you set yourself up to succeed.

You must view the plan for how you will reach your goal as a work in progress. As you come to learn more about what it will take to achieve your goal, you can use this new information to modify the plan. For example, perhaps you go to school with the goal of earning a certificate to become a teacher. By the time you complete your schooling, however, jobs for teachers are tight. So, instead of moving right into teaching elementary school students, as you had hoped, you take a job conducting training in a corporate setting. You don't give up on your original goal, but you learn to adapt and realign your timeline to fit the reality of the situation.

As a therapist, I suggest that my clients set goals for their treatment. Part of that goal-setting is to have them ask themselves how they will know when they have reached their goal. For some goals, this is simple and concrete. If I want a new house, I know I have reached my goal when I purchase my new house. If I have been specific in my definition of the goal, the house has three bedrooms, a great kitchen, space for a studio and study, and is in the neighborhood I want to live in. I can not only smell the roses bushes in the stimuli-enriched creation of my goal, I can look out to where the rose bush will be.

140

What if you find that you haven't reached your goal within the timeline that you have set? The problem may not necessarily lie with the goal, but with the plan to reach that goal. Life holds examples of people who have reached for and attained the same goal. How did they do it? Look around you. Talk to people who have achieved the same goal you seek. How did they do it? Try to determine what they did that you haven't done to create a similar future.

Writing down your goals is an important step in realizing them. Post your written goals where you can readily see them. This simple act of putting your goals into a visual medium is similar to using affirmations. Every time you see them you reflect on where you want to go in your life.

We all have goals that involve long-term rewards. It may be the desire for a better job, a larger house, the mastery of a foreign language, a trip to a far-off place. Attending school with the intention of completing a course of study is a long and difficult process. Students work at a level of high demand to successfully fulfill their academic, professional, and personal obligations. When I was trying to juggle these important aspects of my life, I found myself asking, more than once, "Why the HELL am I doing this!" Having a tangible symbol of my dreams and goals gave me an ongoing reminder of why I was working so hard.

Throughout my schooling I kept a picture of a fishing boat at eye level beside my computer screen. I had set a goal for myself that when I accomplished my retraining, which hopefully would allow me to get a better job and make more money, I would get something for myself that I had always wanted. I would look at that picture of the boat and imagine a time in the future when I didn't have to work so hard and could enjoy some of the benefits of my efforts.

141

I am reminded of an episode of The Simpsons where Homer, the father in the Simpson family, fails at a job change and is forced to return to the drudgery of his old job at the nuclear power plant. He places a picture of his baby daughter, Maggie, on his control panel and says, poignantly, that his child is the reason he endures his job. Like Homer, we all need tangible reminders in our life of just why we work at the level of intensity created by adding school to our already busy lives. Knowing what you are working for helps drive you to complete your education. Use tangible reminders, such as pictures of your kids or your partner or some future dream, in a place where you can see them frequently. When you are working hard, and wondering why, being reminded of your dreams can help tremendously.

Partners and Bringing it All Together

When a person enters school, numerous changes occur, both in the life of the student and the people close

to him. The divorce rate for couples with one partner in
school is very high compared to the general population.
And this statistic doesn't take into account nontraditional
relationships, so there's no tracking for the actual number
of failed relationships as a result of one partner's decision
to go to school.

Oddly, relationships often continue through the
rigors of school only to end soon after school has been
completed and the recent graduate has found the job she
was seeking. In these cases, the couple has grown too far
apart. The relationship has felt inequitable for too long,
positions have become polarized. Each partner may see
the other as unloving and unsupportive—without realizing that the other person may be feeling the same way.

One of the unavoidable outcomes of a person
entering school is that he is not only less physically
available but also less psychologically available. If you
understand this when you commit to an academic regime,
you can avoid some of the pitfalls. Decide early in the
process to set aside time for your family and for your
partner. Make a date to talk about the events of the day,
to spend time laughing, touching, sharing those things
that can easily get lost in the course of a busy week.
Ideally this planning should take place before a person
enters school. Realistically, you will probably need to
make a course correction in how you support one another
through the process. Often a few sessions with a professional counselor can be of enormous help in making some
beneficial changes in a relationship that isn't tracking in a
way that sustains both partners. Think of it as an investment in yourselves.

When you graduate from school, your partner
graduates too. In fact, your partner probably should be the
one getting the graduation presents at the end of the process.
He/she might not have the degree, but he/she has been
through a process. He/she has taken on new roles that has

142

changed her/him too. Continued growth as a couple is essential through the course of school. Plan for it ahead of time and you'll have a better chance of coming out of the experience together.

The story of one partner sacrificing his growth and development so the other partner can go to school is an old one, too often repeated. As one partner experiences new people and events, he/she can grow distant from his/her partner. Resentment builds in the partner not in school, and if a split occurs in the relationship, that partner rightfully feels used. The supporting partner may cease to embrace his/her own growth and stagnation can occur.

It is important for the partner who is not in school to realize that continued growth as a couple involves the growth of not just one partner but both. You can't dream your partner's dreams. You can share in them but they aren't your dreams. You must continue to have your own dreams and support your movement in a direction that fulfills them. School may not be where your dreams lie. Ask yourself what are the growing edges of your life? How do you stimulate and fulfill yourself independent of your relationship with your partner?

143

If you want to maintain, even nourish, your relationship even while you endure the demands of school, then you need to plan to make that happen. I can suggest some ideas that have been known to help.

Feel. Take time for contact. Take time to hold one another. We all need that physical contact. Kisses going out the door are all too often a quick peck on the cheek. If life were to end for either of you, would you want the memory of your last kiss to be that of an impersonal peck? It takes but a moment to make real contact, and it can mean so much.

Love. We all want love in our lives, but what does that really mean? It must start within our own hearts. When you open your heart to increasing the amount and quality of love in your life, you become a source of love. The more love you give, the move love you will receive. Oftentimes, little resentments get in the way of our reaching out. In our petty anger, we wait for our partners (or parents or children) to reach out to us.

The way to be happy is to let go of anger and resentment. Albert Ellis, founder of Rational Emotive Therapy, had a good point. We choose to feel in particular ways. If we hold on to anger, it can grow and take on a life of its own. Small issues take on far more importance than they should. If we choose to be loving, we will receive love in return. Be the first one to reach out. Give flowers or a backrub for no particular reason and without expectation of anything in return. You will receive far more than you give.

If you had one hour to live, who would you most want to be with? No one will live forever. Making love an active part of a relationship involves living in the moment. Live the moments of love in your life in a fully present fashion. Tell each other that you love one another. Show your love in tangible ways. Do the dishes when it's not your turn. Allow your partner to be "right" even if you feel he/she isn't.

A second part to having a relationship survive is a belief that each of you needs to continue to grow. The sense that you are stagnating is a handcuff that bites into your wrists and restrains your movement. The irony is that, like Dorothy in The Wizard of Oz, who had the power to return home at any time, you have the power right now to change your life, your relationships, and your future. A more realistic Dorothy probably would have throttled the Good Witch for not telling her about this power sooner. Don't wait to accept this truth about yourself. Take the steps to explore those growing edges of your life. Brainstorm how you will support your continued growth through this time. Your partner's focus on school might provide an opportunity for you to grow in ways you have never given yourself permission to explore.

Notes

About the Author

Mr. Glade combines careers as a psychiatric nurse practitioner at a major metropolitan hospital, psychotherapist with a private practice, and consultant and public speaker on health issues. His timesaving methods allowed him to earn a nursing and two post-graduate degrees while balancing the demands of a family and full-time employment. He continues to write, both fiction and nonfiction, and still finds time to enjoy camping and fishing with his wife and son.

Photo by: Michael Donnell, Tricksters Crow Studio

Notes

Order Form

Qty.	Title	Price	Can. Price	Total
	Balancing School and Life and Succeeding at Both - George H. Glade	**$13.95**	**$16.95 CN**	
	Shipping and Handling Add $3.50 for orders in the US/Add $7.50 for Global Priority			
	Sales tax (WA state residents only, add 8.6%)			
	Total enclosed			

Telephone Orders:
Call 1-800-461-1931
Have your VISA or
MasterCard ready.

INTL. Telephone Orders:
Toll free 1-877-250-5500
Have your credit card ready.

Fax Orders:
425-398-1380
Fill out this order form and fax.

Postal Orders:
Hara Publishing
P.O. Box 19732
Seattle, WA 98109

E-mail Orders:
harapub@foxinternet.net

Method of Payment:

☐ Check or Money Order

☐ **VISA**

☐ MasterCard

Expiration Date: _____

Card #: _____

Signature: _____

Name_____
Address_____
City_____ State____ Zip_____
Phone (   )_____ Fax (   )_____

Quantity discounts are available.
Call 425-398-3679 for more information.
Thank you for your order!

Notes

Notes

151

Notes

152